caring

Making a Christian Difference

Raymond Johnston

Collins

Marshall Pickering

William Collins Sons & Co. Ltd
London • Glasgow • Sydney • Auckland
Toronto • Johannesburg

First published in Great Britain in 1990 by Marshall
Pickering

Marshall Pickering is an imprint of
Collins Religious Division,
part of the Collins Publishing Group,
8 Grafton Street, London W1X 3LA

Copyright © Margaret Johnston 1990

Printed and bound in Great Britain by
Cox & Wyman Ltd, Reading, Berks.

Foreword

Raymond Johnston is unquestionably one of the most remarkable men I have ever been privileged to know. We worked closely together for six years. He was a true twentieth-century prophet, speaking to both the Church and the nation. I am thrilled that the lectures he gave at the C. S. Lewis Institute in 1980 are now available in book form.

One of the greatest sadnesses of my life was the loss of my dear friend Raymond Johnston. He was a compassionate and clear thinking man, and I am eternally indebted to six years' working alongside him. The ministry of CARE today is built on the firm foundations laid for us by him. This book on caring and campaigning is a permanent legacy of the heart and mind of Raymond, available to us all.

I was privileged in the last six years of his life to know something of the heart and mind of Raymond Johnston. He was a tireless campaigner, touched with the feelings of the infirmities of people in need. This book, based on the lectures he gave at the C. S. Lewis Institute in 1980, captures the tenderness and genius of a man whose untimely death was a great loss to the Evangelical world and those concerned about our social responsibility in society. I wholeheartedly commend *Caring and Campaigning* to you to be read and re-read.

Raymond Johnston will be remembered as one of the great Christian thinkers and reformers of the twentieth century. Sceptical of the confident claims made by the architects of the permissive society of the 60s and 70s, Raymond tirelessly applied a biblical view of human nature to the issues of abortion, pornography, sexuality, embryology, and to the philosophy that underpinned the legislative changes in these areas made by Parliament. His scholarship and grasp of detail illuminated and challenged both Church and State. Consequently, I am delighted that the lectures he gave at the C. S. Lewis Institute are now available in book form.

LYNDON BOWRING

Editor's Preface

In editing Raymond Johnston's work I have attempted to arrive at the text he would have presented to the publishers had he lived to see his manuscript into print. Apart from routine minor editorial corrections, I have silently altered those references which needed straightforward updating; where a social, political or other situation has changed significantly since the lectures were first delivered, I have made appropriate changes and drawn the reader's attention to the changed situation. I have also provided several opening paragraphs for the Introduction, referring to a range of contemporary developments of the kind that Raymond Johnston would have wished to cite.

I am grateful to Dr Nigel Cameron of Rutherford House, Edinburgh, who has kindly read and commented upon the edited manuscript.

DAVID PORTER

Acknowledgements

This book grew out of a series of lectures, given at the C.S. Lewis Institute in Washington DC in 1980. I shall not easily forget the generous hospitality of Dr James Houston of Regent College, Vancouver, who inspired the enterprise, Dr John Bernbaum, who undertook the administration, and the lively group of political aides, administrators, academics, students and others who listened attentively (despite the heat!), questioned me perceptively and thus contributed to my own thinking.

Contents

Introduction

We are entering the last years of the twentieth century, and the next decades will find the Western nations facing major decisions. Nationally and internationally, we shall be charting our way through unknown seas. The need for informed and responsible Christian citizenship has never been greater.

But along with the need have come great and unprecedented opportunities. For example, the field of local, national and global communications is one of many in which enormous progress is being made. In many countries, telecommunications systems are being overhauled and replaced with new technologies such as fibre-optic cables, thus permitting much more sophisticated transmission not only of human conversation but a wealth of computer communications. The implications of such a revolution are profound, comparable to those of the invention of printing, or the recent rise in popularity of personal and desk-top computers.

In the related field of the mass media, much heated debate goes on about issues such as the supra-national nature of satellite television, the intervention of government in broadcasting (held by many in Britain, for example, to be a major threat to the freedom and quality of the media), and monopolizing interests in global broadcasting. Satellite television will transform broadcasting in Britain, and some aspects of the transformation have not been universally welcomed. In America, multiplicity of choice has not led to an improvement in standards – as is demonstrated by the existence of pressure groups such as Action on Children's Television – and public service broadcasting is a minority service.

Yet debates and problems such as these ought not to distract us from the fact that contemporary broadcasting media in the West offer substantial sophistication and freedom.

Many complain – often with considerable justification – about the power of Western press barons. Yet in comparison with many countries in the Eastern bloc we have a press that is open, free, and capable of conveying information and opinion without government-dictated censorship and propaganda. Similarly, the airwaves are open; radio and television play an increasing role in Western life (in Britain only a notional one per cent of all households do not possess at least one television set).

The explosion of mass communications technology, and an expanding mass media, make the Christian contribution to public debate – in theory at least – more accessible. Politicians can be questioned more searchingly, and policies scrutinized more closely and criticized more thoroughly. Sir Robin Day is often mentioned as an example of how British television has shifted from a somewhat obsequious style of interviewing politicians, to a much more confrontational, interrogative style.

And scrutiny or lobbying of those in power is not limited only to professional interviewers. The man or woman in the street can write in, phone in, sign a petition, call a meeting, or make use of several other ways of making a personal statement.

*

And yet internationally, the very size of the problem almost crushes us. For example, in human terms it seems impossible to bring about very much change in the threat to liberty and human values that comes from beyond the Iron Curtain. The impassiveness of Soviet leaders and the inscrutability of Chinese politicians makes any prediction foolish.[1]

All that the West can do in the face of brooding Marxist imperialism is to retain realistic military potential so as to deter attack, while at the same time keeping open doors of communication so as to seek disarmament and perhaps (for we are taught to "hope all things") engender trust.

But the Gulag, the secret police, the beating and banishment of Christians, the psychiatric hospitals and the apparatus of repression will not disappear overnight. We must not forget Solzhenitsyn's *Warning to the Western World* of 1976.

Within Britain, people are just as perplexed. The questions that face us baffle the politicians and the experts. Is capitalism intrinsically evil, or is it neutral? Do all brands of socialism lead to inhuman regimentation? Should we slim down the Welfare

[1.] Raymond Johnston delivered these lectures before the remarkable international initiatives of the USSR's Mikhail Gorbachev and the responses of Western leaders, and before the democratisation process in several Soviet satellite states (and Eastern Europe's rejection of Communism) had developed. It is likely that he would have counselled cautious optimism, while perhaps pointing to events such as the Beijing massacre of students in 1989 as a warning that sometimes, indicators of change can be vulnerable to setbacks.

State? Would the nation profit from a resurgence of private education and private medical provision? Have we retained sufficient protection for human life – before birth and at the eventide of old age? Do we wish to put a curb on genetic engineering? What interest should the State take in the health and permanency of marriage? Where are the limits of offensive speech and print to be drawn? How do we define and protect official secrets? Is it time for the links of Church and State to be severed in Britain, or to be strengthened in the United States? What – if any – are the alternatives to Christian morals? And can they preserve our humanity? What is the proper relationship between law, morality and religion?

It is to some of these questions that this book addresses itself.

However overwhelming the international dimension may be, we can at least cleanse our own stables. Within our democracies, there is much that should and could be put right. Secularization has bitten deep, and its sour fruit in human lives, as well as its intellectual bankruptcy, is now becoming more evident. In both Britain and the USA a new mood is evident, very different from the "soft left" naïvety and moral anarchy of the sixties and early seventies. The heady "Make love not war" slogans are now seen for the childish, empty prattle they really were. Less heady, less optimistic, more doubtful, more pragmatic, the modern mood has a realism which makes it, in principle, more open to Christian reason.

A revival of principled Christian citizenship is now called for. The Christian protest movements of the 1970s did noble work, but they too often stopped short at sloganizing. We need to go further. It is time both for deeper biblical thinking and for much more resolute and organized Christian political involvement.

I

Judging Nations

Our theme is public policy and how Christian morality relates to it. It is a subject that poses questions
about the use of power, the way society is going, the
quality of life and the nature of the social climate in
which we live.

The book progresses from the general to the particular. Indeed, only one assumption is made as we
begin; that the reader has doubts about the wisdom
of Christian social involvement, or about whether
it is either appropriate or in fact possible to make
judgements about social policy. That is the subject
of this, the first, chapter.

In the second chapter we explore the consequences
of failing to promote a Christian involvement in
social policy – of not "blowing the trumpet". And
we do this by outlining a biblical theology of social
involvement.

In the third chapter we address the apparent conflict between equality and compassion – two quests
that dominate discussions of social policy today; and
this involves formulating a biblical definition of the
proper use of governmental power.

Chapter four presents a number of specific issues
under the overall title of "Public policy and the value

of human life": capital punishment, war and peace, the nuclear question, crime and restitution, abortion, infanticide, and euthanasia.

The final chapter discusses the role of public policy in protecting human social institutions or behaviour-patterns, and particularly its role in protecting family values. We conclude by examining ways in which individual Christians and Christian organizations can speak into contemporary discussions of social values, and have an impact on policy-making.

*

Let us begin, then, by considering the feasibility and validity of Christian social involvement and social critique. Such a discussion involves facing four questions.

1. Can we make valid judgements about our nation?

We can, and do, make judgements about our nation. But what makes this a valid exercise? Is it a legitimate one? Three factors suggest that it is.

Firstly, we should note that *most historians have done so*. Irrespective of whether they were Christian or non-Christian historians, they have looked at states and nations as they rose and fell, and at civilizations too. And they have talked of some periods as epochs of glory, and of others as epochs of decadence.

Historians have always spoken not merely in terms of nations' power – of strong countries that conquer, and weak ones that are subjugated – but they have consistently made moral judgements. The Mongols or the Nazis were not simply powerful, they were civil-izations which historians unite to condemn. Pericles'

Athens was not powerful, and yet it was a civilization which historians unite to commend and admire. Even agnostics find themselves compelled to make this kind of judgement, as we see in Sir Isaiah Berlin's famous essay "Historical Inevitability" (1965).[2] Berlin, the Oxford philosopher of the history of ideas, came to the conclusion that the historian is right to praise and to blame. He cannot avoid it. Towards the end of this magnificent essay he writes:

> *Those who are concerned with human affairs are committed to the use of moral categories and concepts which normal language incorporates and expresses. Chemists, philologists, logicians, even sociologists with a strong quantitative bias, by using morally neutral technical terms, can avoid doing so. But historians can scarcely do this. They need not – they are certainly not obliged to – be moral but neither can they avoid the use of normal language with all its associations and "built in" moral categories. To seek to avoid this is to adopt another moral outlook, not none at all.[3]*

The second reason is that *most of us do it anyway, naturally and inevitably*. We talk every day about the budget, or the amount spent on space research, or whether or not we should have a treaty with another country; and immediately we are involved in moral judgements. We say "No" because it's wrong, or "Yes" because it's right. We talk about our nation as going on a right path or going on a wrong path.

The media, too, make such judgements hourly. This is not to say that they are always right or always wrong, for they frequently oversimplify issues. Never-

[2.] Now available in *Four Essays on Liberty* (OUP, 1969; reprinted 1975, 1979).
[3.] Op.cit., p.115.

theless, they contribute to creating an atmosphere where most of us *do* make daily moral judgements about our nation's policies. Nobody rules out all such judgements in principle. It seems that we are all unable to avoid making them.

And in practice, when we get to a certain point we all tend to agree in our judgements. For example, by common consent, genocide and human sacrifice are simply wrong. When we encounter a nation where such things happen, we immediately unite to condemn it. Similarly, we agree that a nation where the judges are incorruptible and the courts are open to all is a nation which has retained, or gained, a worthwhile feature. We will all unite to praise such valuable social institutions, and such judgements are part of our daily existence.

Thirdly, we need to recognize that *moral judgements are uniquely human*. It is *inhuman* to omit the moral dimension when making any observation about a human society. We do not judge animal groups on moral grounds, neither do animals make moral judgements. But we can apply our moral judgements to human groups and individuals, and we are always doing it.

It is a natural and a human thing to do, because human beings are creatures who know good from evil. We are constantly – often with sadness – comparing our expectations of what ought to happen with what actually does happen. To perceive an obligation, that which *should* happen, is a moral awareness which we discover to be part of our very humanity; as C.S. Lewis argued strongly in *The Abolition of Man*, one of the things that makes us truly human is the ability to make moral judgements.[4]

4. C.S. Lewis, *The Abolition of Man* (1943: Collins Fount, 1978), chapter 1.

Can we make judgements about our nation? Yes, certainly we can.

However, there is another question we must ask.

2. Should we make moral judgements about nations?

There are some things which we can do, but do not do, because we say we ought not to do them.

It has often been suggested that some scientific advances have been much too dominated by many scientists' belief that "We can, therefore we ought," but such a belief is not necessarily valid. There may be good reasons for not doing something that is possible in theory. For many people, nuclear fission, nuclear fusion and various aspects of genetic engineering fall within this category.

Yet we certainly *should* make moral judgements about our own community, and there are at least four good reasons for doing so.

Firstly, *human beings learn in social groups*. We are not born with all our values fully developed, and we don't learn them in isolation. In any society, we live among people where certain values are being promoted and other values are being destroyed. Society is always changing, but in that process of change something is constantly being communicated. The culture contains a framework of values.

Because we live in a social group, we need to have some concept of the sort of society we want to become, we need to decide where we ought to be going. What are the danger signs in our society? What remedial action can we take when we see something going in the wrong direction, whether in the sphere of family, school, mass media, or government policies?

Because human beings learn in social groups, it matters what the social group is doing and in which direction it is going. Evaluation is necessary, and that is one reason for making judgements on our own nation. If we acknowledge any communal responsibility at all, we ought to be assessing our condition and our direction.

To this we can add a specifically Christian reason: *God has set individuals in nations*. He has decreed that we should live our existence communally, and in particular in national communities. I have written elsewhere of the balance of unity and diversity that nations display:

> *No individual is "a human being" and no more. We each have our particularity. Secular liberal thinking since the Enlightenment has stressed the rights of each and every person, but abstracts in order to generalize. In this way it misses what is most precious – the unique "I" and the unique "Thou". The class of human beings is a timeless, bloodless intellectual construct, but I am alive here and now. The class would have no significance without its members, each of whom differs significantly from all the others. The reality we know is personal, concrete, individual, irreplaceable. Every person matters, and every person – like every tree or every snowflake – is uniquely "shaped". . . . Any kind of detachment from the idea or the experience of nationhood is impossible by virtue of our human condition. We are born and bred in time and space with a particularity about each one of us. We are men of a given age and culture and we belong to a given community. In our own case we have to reckon with the idea of nationhood which is woven into the texture of Western European thought. This*

*concept is deeply rooted in the history of our
social institutions and our political development
over many centuries. Part of our self-identity is still
expressed by our affirming "I'm English" with the
same meaning and conviction as Shakespeare would
have felt in uttering the same words. It is impossible
for us to stand apart from, or rid ourselves of, the
feeling of national "belonging".[5]*

In Genesis 10 we read how, after the flood, the human
race spread once more over the earth. Over many
centuries each group became distinct in physical
type, historical memory, geographical location and
language. God broke up the human community into
distinctive language groups, signifying the great
cultural differences between nations. This means
that each nation will have its own leadership, its
own responsibilities, its own ways of deciding how
it wishes to develop and how it will move forward.

If God has set us in nations, and if there are
procedures for communally deciding which way our
nation will go, we ought as Christians to pay serious
attention to how decision making takes place in our
society. We are not here by accident. God has put
us here to belong to this country, at this time, by
his sovereign purpose. Christian citizens must take
an active interest in the way in which decisions are
made that decide the direction of our society.

Some Christians are called to be concerned with
this *all* of the time; but all of us have to be concerned
with it *some* of the time. One appropriate time is
when there is an election, for then at least we are
asked to think and help to decide how our nation

5. O.R. Johnston, *Nationhood: Towards a Christian Perspective* (Latimer
Studies 7: Latimer House, 1980), pp. 6–7. That booklet is a fuller
development of the theology of this present section.

should move forward. This is God's decree. Men and women are put in nations, and nations themselves largely decide which way they ought to go.

The third reason why we should make judgements about our own nation is a more solemn one, and it arises from the second.

God judges nations. In the Old Testament, starting with the city-states of Sodom and Gomorrah (which were nations in embryo), then with Egypt and the Exodus, then with Babylon and Nineveh and many other great civilizations in the later prophets – God is judging nations. A most important principle underlying this is found in the book of Jeremiah, where God says to the prophet:

> *At one moment I might speak concerning a nation or concerning a kingdom to uproot, to pull down or to destroy it, if that nation against which I have spoken turns from its evil I will relent concerning the calamity which I intend to bring upon it, or at another moment I might speak concerning a nation or concerning a kingdom to build up or to plant it, if it does evil in my sight by not obeying my voice, then I will think better of the good with which I promised to bless it (Jeremiah 18:7–10; ASB).*

God is constantly building and planting nations, or destroying them. But in every case, he can "change his mind".

We know he does not change his mind in an absolute sense. But *in our experience* his attitude will alter, according to our obedience or disobedience. If a sinful nation, bent upon a path which is clearly evil, turns from its wrongful course, God will (so to speak) change his mind about its eventual destruction. If a nation bent upon a good path changes and becomes corrupt, then he will change his attitude to it so that

8

it will no longer prosper (Jeremiah 18:7).

The principle is therefore that God's judgement is continuous. None of us sees with the certainty of Jeremiah how he is doing it, but he *is* doing it – that is clear from the passage from Jeremiah quoted above. It is not only about Israel, and not only about the sixth century BC. It sheds light on the whole of history. There is a general principle here which still applies: God is judging nations, and he has given us the Bible to discern particular evils and particular goods in nations.

The fourth reason why we should make judgements about our nation is one which Christians have often neglected.

If we do not make judgements, others will. This consideration runs through the argument about religion in schools and many other issues. It is a very powerful argument when thinking about what happens to children in any society: if we do not give the young a basis for telling good from evil, then others will fill the gap. There is no such thing as a moral vacuum. Where Christians are not active, others will very soon move in, and they will often bring very different ideas with them.

I conclude that as Christians we *ought* to be scrutinizing and evaluating our own nation. We must therefore ask our third major question.

3. How should we go about this task?

There are two aspects of the way we go about the task of making moral judgements about our own national community and the policies of society.

The contribution of sociology

Like scientific psychology, sociology is a product of the nineteenth century. The other sciences established themselves much earlier, in the seventeenth and eighteenth centuries, but the human sciences – psychology (the consideration of the individual) and sociology (the consideration of the origins of group behaviour) – are typically the product of the nineteenth century.

"Societies differ," observed the students in this field. "But how do they differ, and why do they differ? How do they change, and why do they change?" The earlier sociologists, like those of today, tried to apply the methods of the physical sciences – empirical data, precise observation, quantification, correlation, theories, models and so on – to total communities.

However, total communities are very difficult things to pin down and examine; so the predictions of the sociologists are often ineffective, and sometimes they are proved wrong. But their descriptive work on short-term developments, particularly those we have seen in our own lifetime, is very important. There is an abundance of evidence on how groups interact with other groups. If God has given us the intelligence to discern this, and the means and the methods to start measuring and quantifying and predicting (or trying to predict) and thus to understand how the pressures of a society work, then surely Christians should pay heed to what is discovered.

Since the Second World War, there has been a tremendous boom in sociology. Books on the subject multiply exceedingly, particularly in the USA! And since there is a social dimension to almost everything that happens, students looking for topics are not short of them.

There are dangers with the sociological approach to human affairs. Firstly, *there is the danger of making developments seem inevitable and deterministic*. When particular social changes are set in a total social pattern, and it is asserted that "This tends to produce that", it looks as if one is saying that there is no need to be concerned with the individual, that there is no such thing as individual freedom, that one person cannot have any effect because the great juggernaut of society rolls relentlessly on.

Secondly, *there is the risk of type-casting*. Sociologists love to categorize things: the "White Anglo-Saxon Protestant", the "typical middle-class white collar worker in a London office", the "Tory voter", and so on. But once people are labelled as members of a group, it can seem that the individual can be ignored and that the group has more reality than the individual. It can seem that what the sociologist is saying is that once you know what a person's income is, how they voted, and what their parents did for a living, you have a total description of them.

Of course we know that this is not the case. Thank God, human beings are all different! But type-casting is a risk and a danger.

Thirdly, there is *the danger of facile optimism*. This attitude, which may be a little more prevalent in America than in Britain, is typified by those who say: "We only need to know just a little bit more, and then we can engineer society and get the answers right." Once the mechanism of social groups and their interaction is understood, it is maintained, we can redesign the whole community. We can programme society to do exactly what we want.

We need to consider these three dangers. Looking first at determinism, it needs to be stressed that a generalization from sociology is only concerned with statistical *probability*. For example, consider the likelihood, or chance, that a person who went to a particular type of school will vote in a certain kind of way. Often the likelihood is as high as ninety per cent – but that is still not a certainty. There are going to be ten per cent who went to the same kind of school but will vote differently.

So only statistical probability can be proposed as a valid sociological principle, and probability is not a thorough-going determinism. Such predictability is what we might expect in any case, exhibiting a certain degree of human regularity in a regular universe. Given consistent character and trustworthiness based on a reliable recurrent pattern of observed behaviour, we should *expect* some degree of prediction to be possible.

But even infallible conviction from complete knowledge would not undermine freedom of choice. This argument has been developed in Professor Donald MacKay's *Human Science and Human Dignity*.[6] In many articles, MacKay has drawn attention to the logical indeterminacy of human choice, showing that even if we *could* predict what a person would do, that would not undermine their actual freedom of choice.

Next we consider the type-casting to which sociology can be prone. Stereotyping is certainly a danger of popular, diffused sociology. One example is "middle-class" as a term of abuse, a usage dating from the late 1960s and denoting something to be sneered at. But there are good and bad aspects to being middle class, and a Christian will want to discern them and to make distinctions.

[6.] Donald MacKay, *Human Science and Human Dignity* (Hodder & Stoughton, London, 1979).

It is very easy to fall into the stereotypes of our own groups, to which we relate most easily. There are, for example, groups for whom the police represent essentially agents of unjust oppression, for whom capitalism is something appallingly evil. Anybody wearing police uniform, or claiming to be a self-made businessman, automatically raises their hackles.

Similarly there are other social groups who are looked upon by some as unable to do anything wrong: the "oppressed masses", or the fighters for social justice in some far-off republic about whom we know next to nothing. They can quite easily be labelled as today's heroes.

Stereotypes such as I have described do obliterate several important distinctions, and Christians must be aware of this, asking, "What is the evidence?", "Is this true of everybody?", "Let's sit down and examine this in detail" – instead of accepting some of the more popular sociological stereotypes.

Next, how do we deal with the optimism built up by some sociologists? This is not an attitude of true sociology at all. On the contrary, much sociology is profoundly pessimistic. It shows how ordinary, apparently strong-minded people can be very easily manipulated. Much sociological research has been devoted to showing how (particularly if you have the media on your side) certain questions are never raised, or certain things are always put in a certain way.

Researchers at Glasgow University have produced two books about how news items are presented on television.[7] They have discovered that industrial

[7.] Raymond Johnston is referring to the work of the Glasgow University Media Group. Typical of their work, and doubtless a book he had in mind, is Peter Beharrell and Greg Philo (eds), *Trade Unions and the Media* (Macmillan, 1970).

disputes in Britain as reported on television always have a certain hidden structure to them, because of the assumptions brought to them by the media men who create the news. Media people often work against the clock, at night in the television studios. But their work always tends to be constrained by the same framework.

That conclusion is very pessimistic, because it shows how easily we can move away from a desire to find the truth, however awkward or irregular it may be, and slip into easy categories handed to us by others. Sociology shows how men can easily fall prey to irrational pressures.

In the 1950s, Orson Welles made a famous radio broadcast based on H.G. Wells's novel *War of the Worlds*. Using plausible imitations of eye-witness accounts and news broadcasts, it realistically evoked a Martian invasion of earth. Many listeners believed that an invasion was actually taking place, and the result was public panic throughout the United States.

The implications of such events are very profound and rather pessimistic.

Yet, despite these dangers, Christians must understand the positive value of sociology. It provides a tool for understanding God's world, and an incentive to question group behaviour. Sociology illuminates social disadvantage, which is something that Christians ought to be concerned about – why is it that members of certain groups can never "make it to the top"? Sociology also illuminates the basic needs of a stable society. Could anything be more important? Family life, moral consensus, an authority structure which is just and open, the importance of education – all come under sociological scrutiny. The sociologist examines the complexity of human relations and human groups. Sociologists can awaken us to the state of the nation and the Church. As Christians, we need to know about the state of the nation in religious terms. We have much to learn from sociology about the state of the Church and its influence in the community. Some sociological research is the work of Christians, bringing an intelligent biblical perspective to bear on the fruits of sociological analysis. That is one aspect of the task of making proper moral judgements about our nation using the data and insights of sociology.

The theological contribution

To the sociological aspect of our task we need to add the theological. We ought to be taking the word of God more seriously. Christian discernment will always bring us back to Scripture. We may need sociology to help us analyse a problem; but when it has done so, then we must come back to Scripture. There can be no certainty about moral judgements from other sources.

Having said that, it must be added that in every society, whether Christianity has established itself there or not, there is a certain area of common agreement. C.S. Lewis's *Abolition of Man* (1943) demonstrates this universal awareness: that lying is wrong, promise-breaking is a bad thing, wanton unprovoked injury to someone else ought to be stopped, stealing is wrong, family loyalty is important.

This is the area that Reformation theologians refer to as that of "common grace". All these emphases are common to most societies and most countries in every age of man. Lewis calls them "the Tao" (a word he takes from Eastern philosophy) or "the primeval platitudes" since these agreed items go back through virtually every civilization. However, there is more

15

than the Tao to the moral character of any particular society.

Every culture has particular things which make it individual, special and different. For instance, it has its own regulations about sexual behaviour, food and eating customs, or about which different racial groups may co-exist and intermarry in that society; it has convictions about cruelty to animals, about what may be done to animals and plant life, about the use of drugs, about the nature and purpose of punishment, about how to dispose of the bodies of the dead, and so on. These are matters which differentiate societies. Priorities differ too between one society and another. How serious, for example, are offences against property, as contrasted with offences against the person? But all these items give societies their distinctive character, despite the fact that they are all sharing the "primeval platitudes" which Lewis talks about.

Perhaps the most important question is: where is the focus for moral aspiration? Where do people look for guidance on values? Where is the moral heart of things?

A moral vision is needed to inspire a people and to give them coherence and identity and purpose, and the dominant moral visions of societies differ. Some – in particular, many of the Eastern religions – cherish the distant possibility of merging with the Infinite. In the West, we have looked for centuries at the picture of a man dying on a cross, giving himself for his fellow men. With that goes the conviction that one day history will come to an end and God will finally judge every human being, the living and the dead. These visions which shape moral beliefs are very different in different societies. But because they determine what we think about the purpose of life, they have tremendous inspirational power. Men share much, by virtue of what the theologians call "common grace"; yet societies differ.

A God-given moral framework exists. So what does the Bible say about this topic?

It is wonderfully clear. On sexual relations, for example, the Bible is explicit about the requirement of chastity before marriage and faithfulness within it. On the welfare of animals, too, there is an amazing amount of legislation in the Old Testament. The society with which God was dealing was a primitive one, but it is extremely moving and very beautiful to see the amount of care that God took to secure justice for animals. There are important principles we can discover too about land use, judicial procedures, hygiene, and many other topics.

Today, the issue of addictive drugs is illuminated by the doctrine of the human body as the temple of the Holy Spirit. Human beings are made in God's image, so anything that comes in and distorts them, takes them over, or makes them dependent in the way that drugs do, must be a very evil and very sinister influence.

The Christian also has particular certainty about the issue of punishment. There is a brilliant study of the subject by C.S. Lewis in his essay "The Humanitarian Theory of Punishment". There he demonstrates that the essence of punishment is that it is *retributive*. Punishment is appropriate for somebody when he or she has done wrong, and because they deserve it. Anything else is actually immoral.

According to the Humanitarian theory, to pun-ish a man because he deserves it, and as much as he deserves it, is mere revenge, and, therefore, barbarous and immoral. It is maintained that the

*only legitimate motives for punishing are the desire
to deter others by example or to mend the criminal
. . . . My contention is that this doctrine, merciful
though it appears, really means that each one of us,
from the moment he breaks the law, is deprived of
the rights of a human being.*[8]

That is the exact opposite of what we are told by
many social workers and a variety of well-meaning
people today. We often hear that it is barbaric to
punish somebody simply because they deserve it!
Punishment, it is maintained, is to make somebody
better, to produce a more socialized individual.

But Lewis explains that if that is our rationale, we
have a fine excuse for taking the offender away and
doing anything we like to him. If the psychologist
says that what criminals need is twenty years in
solitary confinement to make them good citizens,
then – if our sole concern is making them good
citizens – we will put them in solitary confinement for
twenty years. The only thing that could stop us doing
so would be the retributive factor: if we said, "Wait
a moment – that person has done this or that, but he
does not *deserve* twenty years." To say that would be
to assert that twenty years was in no way the right,
fitting, just, morally appropriate punishment for the
deed which he had committed. This is the essence
of Lewis's case: that *only* retributive punishment
preserves justice in penal theory and practice, and
only this approach treats man as responsible.

*

[8] C.S. Lewis, "The Humanitarian Theory of Punishment", *20th Century:
An Australian Quarterly Review*, vol.iii no.3 (1949), pp. 5–12. Reprinted in
e.g., C.S. Lewis ed. Walter Hooper, *God in the Dock: Essays on Theology
and Ethics* (Eerdmans, 1970), p. 287 (quote from that edn, pp. 287–88), and
First and Second Things (Fount Paperbacks, 1985).

So the Bible contains a coherent network of moral principles and priorities for social life. The word of God calls us inescapably to the task of assessing our own nation in the light of this framework. It is not only a legitimate activity; we have the right to do it – and we have the tools to do it. We *must* assess our own nation – and indeed other nations.

But we need to be humble about other nations, since we rarely know as much about what is going on there as we do about our own country. A classic device, employed by many attempting to manipulate our society today, is to take our minds off what we could be doing about something *here*, and to send us out into the streets with great moral indigestion, to condemn something going on in another part of the world about which we know virtually nothing. One powerful television programme can make millions feel incensed, and thousands can be tempted to go out and protest. Young people are particularly at risk here. There are many causes they could work for at home, instead of, for instance, standing outside the South African Embassy thinking that doing so will end apartheid (which is not to say that apartheid is just or tolerable).

The testimony of the Old Testament prophets has not been preserved in vain. Christians are finding today – though painfully late in some cases – that the Old Testament contains much teaching that, with suitable translation, can and should be applied to our society.

There is a serious ignorance of the Old Testament in our churches today and some young people hardly ever open it, though they are familiar with the gospels and epistles. The whole of Jesus's ministry was saturated in the Old Testament, with references to every part of it. For those who value the renewed emphasis on the work of the Holy Spirit in the Church today, one fact is especially significant: the first Christian sermon preached under the influence of God the Holy Spirit was simply a chain of Old Testament quotations. That is what the Holy Spirit did at Pentecost.

If that is so, then perhaps there is more for us to learn from the Old Testament than most of us realize. In the past three decades, an increasing number of Christians have been struggling back to the great moral certainties that gripped our Puritan ancestors in seventeenth-century Britain. Forced out of England by religious intolerance, those men – the Pilgrim Fathers – have been deeply influential down the centuries in Western culture on both sides of the Atlantic.

4. How do we approach and assess public morality?

In every nation the background to public policy – what a nation decides to do – is public morality.

Policy is limited, if not determined, by what a nation believes on the whole to be right. Public morality is a shared system of moral ideals which guides conduct. Public as well as private behaviour is shaped by communally shared patterns of values.

Public morality may be discerned in various ways of which I would mention two. It is indicated "officially" by the standards enshrined in the laws of the land, and by the codes of behaviour established for professions, trades and other groups. If we look at the codes of practice for advertisers or for doctors or for employers and then at the laws of the land, the totality of laws and codes will give us some idea of the structure and content of a society's public morality. It is also indicated by what people actually *do* to help or to harm, edify or to destroy, their fellow citizens. This takes us to the statistics of crime, of benevolent activity, of deviance and public health. Thus public morality is both what men say they *ought* to do and also what they actually *do* do.

These indicators may be described as "official" ways of looking at the morality of a society. But other ways exist, which are just as important but less clear-cut. Nevertheless, they are significant because they hint at the moral climate of a nation.

What can people say and "get away with" in the communication system? What would a television commentator be allowed to say and what he would not be allowed to say? The answers to such questions provide a real indication of what the moral climate is. Of course, it will change, and in Britain we have watched it change quite remarkably in the last twenty years. Again, we might ask: What can somebody get away with, without risking his job or his local reputation? There has been a tremendous change here, particularly as regards marital and sexual behaviour. Many of the most flagrant breaches of God's law (or, to use a secular expression, many types of destructive sexual behaviour) can be indulged in, and the man or woman concerned can say that an employer has no right to dismiss him or her for such behaviour, that it is part of one's "private life". Very often, such statements have considerable legal weight.

These conventions of how we assess behaviour are indications of what people can "get away with", and of how the moral climate is moving. We need to note what makes people ashamed, and what can they do blatantly without any fear of shame at all. Our own moral climate is very confused, on both sides of the Atlantic. It is a new Babel. Does this matter?

Surely, when there is a Babel in morality, there is cause for concern. We are rightly worried by the sort of behaviour that our children are being taught in schools. In addition, we have gross materialism; public morality in both Britain and the USA is extremely materialistic. Constant attention is focused on wages and the economy. The industries that are booming are consumer durables and entertainment – those associated with a materialistic society. They produce goods which appeal to the body rather than to the soul. Self-indulgence and addictive habits are prevalent. The alcohol and tobacco industries in Britain are prospering. Pop stars and sportsmen are paid much more than the Prime Minister. Superstitions flourish, and so do every kind of magic and occult experimentation – such as horoscopes, spiritism and experiment with the supernatural. In Britain today, Satanism is widespread.

This is a tremendous shift to have taken place over the last twenty years. In the 1950s there was no public network of deviance such as there is today. We are told that this is an age of reason; but the reality is that we are in an age of superstition. We have emerged from an ecclesiastically dominated culture, yet we seem to be moving into something much worse. Occult religions are cruel, exploitative and dehumanizing. We also live in a violent society in which crime statistics stand at a frightening level on both sides of the Atlantic. Yet we feed our minds and those of our children nightly on more and more televised violence. Confused, materialistic, superstitious and violent – such is the moral climate of the 1980s. How do other people see us?

In 1976, after that great Russian writer Solzhenitsyn

finally left his native land, a land which he loved and still does love dearly, he said:

> *It is with a strange feeling that those of us who come from the Soviet Union look upon the West of today. It is as though we were neither neighbours on the same planet, nor contemporaries – and yet we contemplate the West from what will be your future, or look back seventy years, to see our past suddenly repeating itself. And what we see is always the same as it was then: adults deferring to the opinion of their children; the younger generation carried away by shallow worthless ideas; professors scared of being unfashionable; journalists refusing to take responsibility for the words they squander so profusely; universal sympathy for revolutionary extremists; people with serious objections unable or unwilling to voice them; the majority passively obsessed by a feeling of doom; feeble government, societies whose defensive reactions have become paralysed; spiritual confusion leading to political upheaval. What will happen as a result of all this lies ahead of us. But the time is near and from bitter memory we can easily predict what these events will be.*

Most of this diagnosis was right – perhaps all of it, to some degree. What can be done? What *should* be done? To that we shall turn in the following chapters.

II

On Not Blowing the Trumpet

We have seen that Christians *can* make judgements about their nation, and indeed that they *should* do so. Admittedly it is a difficult and demanding task, and we need to employ insights and knowledge from those who study societies, and particularly our own society. We have seen that sociology has its advantages and its dangers, but that it has its proper use; and that we also need authentic Christian theology fashioned out of biblical teaching. With this we can forge an evaluative framework for an assessment of what is going on in society around us.

We must come now to sketch out a Christian theology of social involvement. It is a solemn responsibility, as Ezekiel reminds us when he speaks about the watchman's duty to blow the trumpet when he sees danger (Ezekiel 33:6).

I

We must start, however, by examining the case which can be made *against* social involvement by Christians. We should do justice to this case, before we go on to refute it.

Many of our parents and grandparents would have

known this case very well. Believing in its validity, they might have warned us: "Do not go into politics; have nothing to do with this dirty game; you will get your hands soiled!" And then to support this view, they would have brought in texts which are indeed in the Bible.

We must listen to them before we do anything else.

The negative position has a respectable lineage. It goes right back to the early centuries of Christianity, when some of the holiest Christian men in Egypt withdrew from society, went to sit in caves (or, in a few cases, on the top of pillars), and so retired completely from the world. The monastic movement later brought some of them together into small communities, but still they were essentially separate. The same attitude towards the world can be traced down through the history of the Church. Many movements of fine Christian men and women in the last century felt that their allegiance to Christ meant that they should withdraw from society, and they acted accordingly. This conviction is sometimes, perhaps unkindly, stigmatized as a "ghetto mentality", and is still with us today. But what does it preserve that is genuinely Christian?

Firstly, *it does justice to the New Testament warning that there is a deep evil in the world order*. The apostle John tells us (1 John 5:9) that the whole world lies in the control of the evil one. This is a fallen planet; we live in a darkened world. Ours is, in C.S. Lewis's words, the "silent planet", the planet on which all other creatures in the universe look down, beholding it shrouded in darkness and mist. Communication with the Creator has been lost and it is a rebel world, alienated from the source of all goodness. If a New Testament writer can say that the whole world order lies in the power and the grip of the evil one, then clearly here is the beginning of a case against involvement. The world is so bad that we should contract out!

Secondly, *"God has delivered us from the dominion of darkness and transferred us to the kingdom of his beloved son"* (Colossians 1:13) – hence the glorious feeling of deliverance which Christians have when they are converted. In particular, those who experience a sudden conversion in which everything becomes new have an immediate reaction against old habits, old friends, old institutions, and the way they used to run their lives. There is a great tendency for such people to stress the essential difference between the sort of life they now feel called to live, and the life they were living before. This leads them to say (using texts such as Philippians 3:20), "Our citizenship is in heaven: that is where I really belong. What use to me are the institutions of this world, now that I am a different and a new person?" Social involvement, surely, belongs to the barren and ineffective struggle in which the unconverted, with eyes only for this world, engage.

Thirdly, consider *the pilgrim image*. The Christian life is that of an alien upon the earth. As Hebrews 13:14 puts it, we have here no continuing city. Hebrews 11 is never tired of stressing the fact that the children of God are not at home here below. This is not really where we belong; the New Testament constantly warns that we are not to feel too deeply entrenched in this earth.

Fourthly, there are *the dangers of contamination*. James 1:25 urges us to keep ourselves "unstained and unspotted" from the world. In Jude 23, the image is of the Christian saving somebody else – but taking great care not to get burnt by the fire out of which

27

he is snatching others. Those whom you are helping to Christian faith are like lepers, Jude explains; they have a disease. You must save them, but be careful that you do not catch that disease.

*

Such are the basic arguments of the case against Christian involvement in society, or the communal life of this world; and particularly against any kind of political involvement.

But none of them close the question. The verses quoted are rightly taken seriously, and the attitudes are correctly discerned. There *are* risks and dangers. But risks and dangers do not negate positive things that the Bible tells us, which alter the picture.

I hope I have been fair to the negative case, because many of our ancestors would have deprecated the very idea of having any kind of political job, or standing for election to any kind of public office. Many of them would not even have used their vote, because they would have said that the whole business was unutterably tainted.

II

We turn now to the positive case for Christian involvement, and the first consideration is this:

God is still sovereign in his world

Ephesians 1:12 tells us that God is still working all things according to his will. Everything that happens is under his control. This includes the destiny of the nations, as Psalm 67:4 reminds us: "Thou dost judge the nations with equity and guide the nations upon earth." Would it not seem very strange, if the God who is sovereign and who is in control of nations should say to his own people "But you must not have anything to do with *this*, of course!"?

The first thing the Christian sees is that *his God is concerned with guiding the nations*. Public office for the child of God is not ruled out – rather, this doctrine establishes a *prima facie* case for it.

Secondly, *man still remains a steward*, held responsible and accountable to God for the power and the influence which he is given as vice-regent of the created order. Genesis 1:28 speaks of this dominion, and Genesis 2:15 amplifies it in terms of tilling and keeping the garden. In other words, man rules and cares for this world under God. If that is so, then this must include community responsibility, because part of the way we take care of the world is through political and social means, through institutions and groups. Community responsibility means, among other things, the laws that are made, the resources that are sought for and discovered, and the use that is made of them. Men and women cannot exercise that stewardship unless they are involved in the mechanisms of society. Even after the fall, the mandate was not revoked.

Thirdly, *the servant of God who knows what social righteousness is has a duty to proclaim it*. Ezekiel 33:6 speaks of the blood-guilt of God's people. We carry a heavy burden of guilt if we do not guide our fellow citizens away from danger, and towards stability, happiness and security.

Ezekiel is referring primarily to the proclamation of God's revealed will. If that revealed will contains teachings about how people should be living in society, then that must be part of what we too are supposed to be proclaiming.

Fourthly, *Jesus left us in the world and did not take us out of it*. He gave us no instructions to contract out of social responsibility, but instead he prayed that we might be kept from Satan (John 17:15). Conversion does not project us out of this world, it leaves us here on earth – with our eyes open: in the world, but not of it, and kept from Satan.

This is the prayer that should especially encourage us to pray for Christians who hold responsible positions in government. Jesus has put them there too, and we must pray that his power will keep them from the many insidious temptations to which they are exposed.

Fifthly, *there is the evidence of Matthew 5:13 and 16*. These well-known verses emphasize that Christians must let their light shine before the eyes of their fellow citizens, so that the latter may "see their good works" and thank God for them. Christians are to be salt in the world, said Jesus. To be effective, salt must be sprinkled on food, it is no use if it is left in the salt cellar.

For centuries, salt has been rubbed into food to preserve it, and that is how it has to be used, if it is to achieve its preservative effect. In the same way, Christians must be "rubbed" into their society, so that God in his mercy might have a "preservative effect" upon the goodness and righteousness which still exist in that community. Take out the salt, and there will be a decline in the preservative power.

Some expositors believe that the use of the salt image relates more to the matter of what food tastes like. Salt makes the difference between a flavoursome, tasty meal and a dull and bland one. But the analogy holds. If the flavour of our communal life is to keep a good and wholesome flavour which people will enjoy, then Christians must permeate society and exercise a wholesome influence.

Let me illustrate what I mean. One could use honesty, integrity, cheerfulness, reliability, or fair dealing – all characteristics by which a Christian spreads light and goodness – but let me instead use a less obvious "virtue": the influence of a lively sense of humour. A Christian who has no sense of humour should pray for one! And those who rejoice in such a gift should pray that the Lord will help them to use it to good advantage. Humour is a priceless gift in many a tense meeting and many a fraught confrontation in political, industrial and ecclesiastical situations. It is part of "being salt" in the common room, staff room, canteen, board room or office.

Matthew 5:16 and 1 Peter 2:12 both remind us that people need to see our good deeds. That means we must be around in the market place, in the shop or in the office – wherever our social situations take us – actively pursuing goodness. If we were to be taken out of worldly society into a self-contained, exclusively Christian community, our fellow-citizens would never see our good deeds.

Sixthly, *we must note the influential godly civil servants in Scripture*. In the Old Testament we come across two important civil servants, holding high office in pagan governments: Joseph and Daniel.

In fact, they were even more than civil servants. Pharaoh presented Joseph with the traditional symbols of high government office (Genesis 41:41–43), and there are several indications, in the Genesis account of his later career, that Joseph had the status and responsibilities of what we would today call a politician. Daniel, living in a similarly autocratic society, held government posts under three successive heads of state and seems to have been a politician rather than merely a favoured servant (e.g.

Daniel 5:29). Without these men, their nations would have been in very difficult positions. In the one case, the nation would have been wiped out by a severe famine, or at least decimated. In the other, God-given wisdom concerning certain future political events was brought to the Head of State himself by Daniel. Even the most cursory reading of the lives of Joseph and Daniel shows how each of these two servants of God brought blessing to the nation.

Those detailed histories are not in the Bible by chance. They are there to encourage Christians to be ready to move to the very top of the political and social ladders in their own countries. Not all Christians will receive such a calling, of course, but *some* may be called to fill these positions, and they may do so with confidence, because of what God did through Joseph and Daniel.

Perhaps some of the secularist and dehumanizing tendencies in Britain and North America today would never have taken such deep root if we had had more young Christians willing to aim for the top in political life, and to do so without compromise. They could have surrounded some of our Presidents and Prime Ministers with a Christian atmosphere from the very start. In Scripture two men were called to do this: Joseph and Daniel.

Seventhly, *Scripture offers us a model community from which to learn.* God once organized a whole nation – Israel.

To adopt a model does not always mean that you follow it in every particular and every detail. Only infrequently can we take a particular Old Testament law and apply it, completely in its original form, to our own situation, but clearly we are meant to learn some principles from the Old Testament. The offences God cannot tolerate, those things that will inevitably lead to disaster in family or community, are underlined time and time again. Every community is a moral community, having and needing explicit values. This inevitably implies that Christians, taking the guidance they find in the life of Israel, can be led into positive and principled social involvement.

Eighthly, *we are commanded by the Apostle Paul to pray for good government* (1 Timothy 1:2–4). How could we conceive that God would ask all his people to pray for something, and then respond by saying that of course, the answer can only come through the ungodly?

God is going to cause some of us to become the answer to our own prayers; he is going to call *some* of us, at least, into positions of political and social influence. Where the good laws and the just order for which we pray are determined and implemented, there will be some Christian people there helping to make the decisions. We must all pray, but some of us will actually be called to actualize the answers to these prayers.

Ninthly, *we should note Galatians 6:10.*

Therefore, as we have opportunity, let us do good to all people, especially to those who belong to the family of believers.

This applies particularly to those of us living in democracies. In a genuine democracy, every citizen has some power to change things, a power that can be used sometimes, if only through the ballot box when voting. However, usually citizens of a democracy have many other opportunities as well. As soon as we have that power – our democratic "rights" bestowed by God in his providence – we have what Paul here calls "opportunity". And so much as we have opportunity, says Paul, we are to do good *to all men*, and especially the household of faith. Democracy means that we have opportunities – and we are meant to use them.

Finally, the case for social involvement is completed by a solemn warning. *Doing nothing has its own sad results.* If Christians become complacent – for example, if they abstain from voting or using their social influence – they are like salt without savour. This can only mean that evil will gain control more easily.

The Bible mentions one man (he was the High Priest at the time) who had a chance to apply God's standards, but failed to do so. The infant Samuel was finally sent to him to announce God's terrible message of rejection of Eli and his family from the priesthood. "I am about to punish his house for ever, for the iniquity which he knew, because his sons were blaspheming God, and he did not restrain them" (1 Samuel 3:13). If the Christian knows of an evil and has the power to restrain it, then he must do so.

This terrible warning completes what is surely a conclusive case for Christian social involvement. Scripture leaves us in no doubt on the matter.

III

There is, however, a further dimension to our Christian duty, and we must consider it before we go on to talk about details.

The word of God challenges us about our *motives*.

There is a theology of motives in the New Testament, and it has at least four aspects. If we are simply seeking the gratitude of men for example, and wanting the applause of the crowd, then that is wrong. That was the unworthy motive of many of the Pharisees (Matthew 1, 5, 16). But the Christian strives only to deserve the appreciation of God. How is that achieved? How do we ensure that ours is social involvement of the kind that merits God's "Well done, good and faithful servant!"? There seem to be four motives indicated in the New Testament.

Firstly, *to be like our heavenly Father himself*. In two words: unselective benevolence. In Matthew 5:45 we read that God sends his rain and his sun on "the just and the unjust". Rain and sun are two things absolutely necessary for life. Without them there would be no warmth and no food. Yet God sends them to us, irrespective of what we deserve, whether we are Christians or non-Christians. In the Sermon on the Mount, Jesus challenges us to be unselective in our doing of good in just the same way.

Our first motive is therefore rooted in our natural desire that we should be like our heavenly Father. That means being unselective, doing good to all those who come within our range of influence.

Secondly, *to obey the express command of God*. In Matthew 22:39 Jesus sets us the standard of simply loving our neighbours as ourselves. Our unselective love *must* be available for needy individuals.

The good Samaritan showed this in action. The two men in the story were separated by religion and partly by race. Certainly they were unknown to each other. Nevertheless, the man who saw the need did good to the man who was in that dire need. God commands that whenever we see someone whom we can help, we should do so. Loving one's neighbour is practical, disinterested caring. This command will help us to avoid political stridency, which is an ever-present danger. Is our motive real love? If it is, then somehow or other that will come over in everything we say, and our tone – even when we are asserting

35

"We must stop this" – will be perceived as one of sorrow and love.

A Christian must not be seen as somebody who brandishes power in order to stop something, and rather enjoys doing so. We must be sure that our motives for exercising power are obedience to our heavenly Father, and love for our neighbour.

Our third motive is *to demonstrate the reality of grace and faith*, and here the New Testament evidence is rich indeed. We ought to soak ourselves in three entire chapters: the third and fourth chapters of 1 John and the second chapter of James. The two chapters of 1 John revolve around love, and how love must be demonstrated in action, and similarly the second chapter of James revolves around faith, and how faith must issue in action.

The watching world has every right to doubt our testimony if it does not see love and faith in action. If our fellow-citizens do not see loving social involvement, then they have every right to say, "That religious bunch are phoney"; we have given them every excuse for saying that the Gospel is irrelevant.

Our fourth motive must be *to use the gifts that God has given us*. Daniel and Joseph were men to whom God gave gifts of wisdom and leadership – then he almost pushed them into the positions they had! Their response was not to attempt to run away, but instead, they resolved to shoulder that responsibility; and the insight of Joseph and the wisdom of Daniel were used to bless a whole society.

But perhaps the best-known biblical source for this motive is a passage in the book of Esther. Very remarkably, Esther's beauty appears to have been used to raise her from obscurity into the fifth-century equivalent of the Cabinet Office, and in that place to influence political events towards justice for God's people and towards goodness. A well-known verse in Esther records Mordecai's words to her: "Who knows whether you have not come to the kingdom for such a time as this?" (Esther 4:14).

Sometimes God gives us an opportunity, or a particular gift. Joseph, Daniel and Esther had gifts that took them to positions of influence. Christians should be asking themselves whether *their* gifts are such that possibly one day they will be sent for and asked to do a job which is politically or socially sensitive, or difficult or demanding. Such an invitation may raise questions in our mind: "Will I be able to go there and shine for Christ?"; "Can I avoid compromise?" The answer is, surely, "Yes, you can".

Is there any Commission or Enquiry on which a Christian might be asked to serve, and on which he or she ought to refuse to do so? No. So many Christians in Britain have withdrawn from social involvement, that the setting up of a Government Commission or Departmental Enquiry on almost any topic highlights the scarcity of Christians who are skilled, well-read and articulate. When the civil servants draw up the lists, Christians are not there. In seeking to change this, we are not simply aspiring to gain influence, but rather acknowledging that God has given gifts to his children. In seeking change, we acknowledge that if we have a gift in a particular area, and if we are offered a position of social influence to use that gift, then we should accept.

Such an approach will keep us humble. When we talk of gifts, our mind is on the Giver. That attitude will keep our motives right. And to be effective, we *must* discern and retain these genuine motives for Christian social involvement.

IV

Our obligation is clear and our proper motives are established. We can now turn to strategic considerations, and here again good theology can help us.

First of all, *New Testament priorities must be retained in the Church*. No Christian should be allowed to forget that he or she is a member of a church, whatever his or her social responsibilities.

Church decisions within the fellowship have to make Church priorities clear to the world. The first task of the Church in the world is to preach the Gospel. The major thrust of the New Testament suggests that the greater part of every Christian's time and money should be given to evangelism and to building up the people of God. Any church taking the New Testament seriously must bear this priority in mind.

This is not to say that churches may not set individuals aside to do other things. We have Metropolitan, County and District Councils in Britain who are responsible for many of the services in a local area – for example, education, roads, social services; and any public-spirited citizen who is a resident and ratepayer can, if he or she wishes, stand for election to the local council. Often, being elected to the council is the beginning of a political career. It is voluntary, part-time work, but could later lead to a position of even greater responsibility. If there are young people in our churches who say that they are thinking of standing for the local council, will they be prayerfully encouraged – or will they be discouraged? If such a person were a Sunday School teacher would we consider releasing him or her from Sunday School duties?

Do our churches have a positive attitude towards local government responsibility? Do we say: "We will set you aside to do this, and we will pray for you. You must come back to the prayer meeting to tell us what your needs are and we will support you?" Not every Christian will be called in this way, because the major thrust of the Church is to evangelism. That is the apostolic priority, and we must never lose it. Nevertheless, churches should surely set *some* individuals aside in this way.

Our strategy in the Church should also be determined by the fact that *love of God comes before love of neighbour*. This is a clear New Testament priority: Creator before creature. It is a priority that stresses the centrality of worship, both public and private.

The Parliamentarian William Wilberforce felt the need to be constantly reminded that his work should be soaked in prayer and refreshed by the worship of God. Amid all the comings and goings of Parliamentary life, worship alone can purify and refresh. This necessary emphasis sets social action firmly in a church context and a proper Christian framework of life and thought. We must always be asking ourselves, "Where is our love of God in all this activity?"

Another New Testament priority for the Church is found in the apostolic reminder that in the individual's active life of goodness, *if* there is a conflict, *the duty to do good to the household of faith comes first* (cf. Galatians 6:10). We are to "do good to all men"; but – especially where time and resources are limited – the needs of those in the fellowship come first. In terms of local responsibility and the smallest fellowship, the same principle applies: the family comes first (1 Timothy 5:8). There Paul talks very strongly about what the priorities should be when believers have limited resources. The family is our first responsibility: "If any one does not provide for his relatives, and especially for his own family, he has disowned the faith and is worse than an unbeliever." So we are not allowed to put political responsibility before our family.

Here lies a real tension for our politicians. Christian politicians need special understanding and prayer, since they spend much time away from home, and their families come under considerable strain. Perhaps people who are genuinely called to high office are given special strength to do without family relationships for longer than most of us. But we should not assume this to be so in every case. The usual chain of priorities is from family to church to public duties.

*

From New Testament priorities in church and family life, we turn secondly to the vexed topic of biblical priorities in public policy itself. Christians here have been given no blue-print, and the priorities we can discern do not form a comprehensive all-inclusive pattern. Some of our Puritan ancestors on both sides of the Atlantic appear to have thought that they did. From time to time they found themselves in difficulties, took legislation from the Bible and tried to apply it unmodified to their own situation. But the Bible does not contain a *total* pattern of social obligations, with answers to questions on every conceivable matter of duty and relationships. Instead it gives us basic principles to work on. So Christians with their Bibles have to steer a very difficult path. They are not utopians, claiming to possess a complete package of social prescriptions from the Bible, which, if people will only obey it, will make everything perfect. But neither do Christians claim that the Bible tells us nothing at all about social life. We have to steer a course between those two positions.

We begin by stressing the New Testament's undeniable exhortations in favour of civil obedience: Romans 13 and 1 Peter 2:13 simply echo Judges 21:25. Nothing can be more godless and more destructive of our common humanity than a condition in which social authority breaks down and "every man does what is right in his own eyes". Numerous texts in Old and New Testaments present this huge presumption in favour of the godly man being law-abiding. Jesus was unjustly dragged before Pilate and the Sanhedrin, the very Son of God – but he offered no protest.

A recurrent theme in the Acts of the Apostles is the occurrence of civil disobedience and riot. But it is emphatically not the Christians who start it. Some even think that Luke wrote Acts as a kind of justification to the Empire, showing that the Christians were not the ones who started the civil strife which erupted wherever the Gospel went. Wherever social order breaks down, you will find that the cause is either the jealousy of the Jews or secular envy, such as vested interest from the unions, as was demonstrated at Ephesus, where the people who made the images of Diana found their trade dwindling. The Christians, by contrast, lived quietly and obediently. Their principle is most clearly stated in 1 Peter 2:13: "Be subject for the Lord's sake to every human institution." The apostle starts with the emperor, and then moves to the governors under him. So there is good theology behind civil obedience. The theology of Romans 13 undergirds the Petrine principle.

This is not to say that there is never cause for protest. Sometimes there may even be a case for peaceful civil disobedience if the protesting citizen is willing to suffer the consequences. Occasionally we even try to make special provisions for principled dissent; the English-speaking democracies of Britain and North America rightly make provision for conscientious objection, for example, from military service. Francis Schaeffer has argued the case[10] that when you are confronted with extreme evil, or when some policy which you believe to be utterly non-Christian is being foisted upon you, you may be obliged to take the path of disobedience. You must also be prepared to suffer the consequences, whatever the penalty society may decide to attach to this act of disobedience. This of course is itself a kind of obedience, because the Christian is submitting to the whole system. He is professing that he is willing to suffer whatever penalty society determines, but he is also stating that he cannot go along with what society is expecting of him. Such action must be peaceful, honest and humble.

We enjoy the tremendous blessing of a law-abiding society, even though the law is not perfectly just and perfectly fair in all cases. We enjoy it because an ordered social life is more tolerable than anarchy. Judges 21:25 comes at the end of a book which is full of iniquity, immorality, unfaithfulness. It is a terrible book in many ways, and right at the end come these words: "In those days there was no king in Israel; every man did what was right in his own eyes." That is Scripture's comment on anarchy.

The Bible has an inbuilt preference for an ordered society, considering order to be preferable to anarchy. So the rule of law is validated in Scripture. The

[10.] Notably in Francis A. Schaeffer, *A Christian Manifesto* (Crossway Books, Illinois USA, 1981; Pickering and Inglis, UK, 1982), pp. 103–116 ff. [For this British edition of an American book, Raymond Johnston contributed an extended introduction setting Dr Schaeffer's thesis into a British context.]

alternative is the jungle, where the fittest and the strongest prevail, and the weakest are exploited. The rule of law collapses when a central, ordered authority acknowledged by the majority has broken down. The law may be very fallible and faulty, but only when it is taken away do you realize what its value really was. This is the corollary of civil obedience.

Far more can be said, however, about the biblical view of a just and good society. Hosea introduces us to social righteousness as the prophets discovered it, in a crucial passage.

Hear the word of the Lord, O people of Israel;
for the Lord has a controversy with the inhabitants
    of the land.
There is no faithfulness or kindness,
and no knowledge of God in the land;
there is swearing, lying, killing,
    stealing and committing adultery;
they break all bounds and murder follows murder.
Therefore the land mourns,
and all who dwell in it languish,
and also the beasts of the field,
and the birds of the air;
even the fish of the sea are taken away.

(Hosea 4:1–6).

One passage is clearly in the prophet's mind; the echoes are impossible to mistake. His guide to social righteousness is the Ten Commandments. First Hosea says that the general virtues are lacking, there is no faithfulness or kindness. There indeed is a beautiful description of what a humane society means – care and kindness, integrity and faithfulness, where people pledge their word and keep to it. There are the qualities which characterize relationships in a happy society. But in the next verse Hosea goes on to pinpoint more exactly what is going wrong, in terms of specific evils; and there is only one yardstick that the godly man can use. Swearing, lying, killing, committing adultery, stealing, murder after murder – these are transgressions of the third, ninth, sixth, eighth and the seventh commandments.

When the Christian observer wants to put his finger on social unrighteousness, he naturally and rightly turns to the Ten Commandments. These enable us to get to grips with particular evils in society, against which God has set his face. God's children must testify to the good things which are protected and the goodness which is preserved by the moral law of the Ten Commandments. Christians must act as light to expose the breaking of God's law, and salt to disinfect and purify any society where these things begin to spread. These are biblical priorities.

I was once asked during a radio interview whether I thought Christians were often negative in their social witness, always saying "No" and constantly trying to stop people from expressing or enjoying themselves. I agreed that that was sometimes the case, and I did not need to apologize for it, since God gave us a whole group of negatives in the Commandments.

In fact, they are not all negative. There are the positive duties towards God, and there are the obligations to honouring your father and your mother and to keeping the Sabbath day holy. Nevertheless after that comes a whole series of "nots". There are some warnings which come crisp and clear; God forbids certain activities. Yet a negative is merely the reverse side of a positive. The Commandments protect good and beautiful things. One can rephrase them. "Thou shalt not murder" can be rephrased as "Thou shalt respect and regard as holy the image of God in the life of every other man" – life is a sacred thing. "Thou shalt not commit adultery" becomes "Thou shalt respect thy neighbour's marriage" – marriage as God gave it us is a bond between husband and wife which is meant to exclude all others. Every one of God's positives has a negative which protects it. Bible negatives can all be rephrased for discussion and debate in this way.

A good friend of mine answers the charge of negativity by saying: "I am negative about con-centration camps. Aren't you?" There is only one thing you can say about a concentration camp – and that is "No". The reason why the Allies fought the last war was that it was necessary to say "No" to inhumanity of that kind. Negatives are built into any caring human life. God used negatives and so must we.

These Commandments are the biblical priorities, rooted in the changeless prescription of the moral law, good for man as man. They belong to human life as it is meant to be lived, coming as they do from the Creator himself. They are like warning notices at the top of a cliff, or at the edge of treacherous quicksands. These specific biblical negatives cry out to us: "Go no further along that path – it will lead you to disaster."

*

If the Church of Jesus Christ, or indeed the individual Christian, ceases to proclaim God's righteous stand-ards and the inevitable ruin which follows upon disobedience, we are being cruel and unloving to our fellow human beings. They may look at us one day and say: "You *knew*, and you didn't warn us!"

We will have been guilty of not blowing the trumpet.

III

On Justice and Mercy

The quest for equality and compassion in social policy

At this point in our discussion we are in a position to examine more closely Christian options for social policy. In particular, we need to confront the apparent conflict between two ethical ideals, each of which is often taken as the dominant – or even the sole – guiding principle in political debate. They are the two great virtues which (according to Micah 6:8) comprehend all that God requires of man – justice and mercy. Discussions of social policy today are still dominated by the quest for equality and compassion, and appeals to both have become commonplace.

If either, or both, are proposed as basic objectives for active Christians, there is a question we must first address concerning the proper functions of the State: How does a Christian define the use of governmental power?

On this issue, Christians share some common ground with the traditional political philosophers. They hold that justice and mercy are the two things that the State, whatever else it does not do, is bound to provide for those who are born into it and are

47

therefore involuntary members of it. They hold that the State is that aspect of our social organization which is vested with sole coercive power. The legitimate use of physical force, and of the lesser types of coercion (for example financial penalties, such as taxation and fines), are vested in the State. In return, the State assumes two basic responsibilities for all citizens.

The first is *to protect the people, the territory, and the property of those it represents*. English law speaks of the duty of "protecting us against the Queen's enemies". Another ancient phrase is "the safety of this realm". The State must protect the citizens from external attack. We order things in this way, so that we may communally enjoy together an adequate degree of protection as a nation and as a community.

The second function of the State is equally obvious, and is a political duty discerned equally by most other political thinkers, Christian or non-Christian. *Individuals within the community may need to be protected from each other*. In their person or in their property, they need defence against any unwarranted intrusion or harm. Every life and limb is afforded a degree of protection by the State, and so is any property which the individual citizen might possess.

Here, too, the use of coercive power is a possibility. In terms of the actual organs of government power, we have the armed forces for the first function of the State, and the police, the courts of justice and the prisons for the second. The armed forces protect the state or community against external attack, while the police and the courts, in a slightly different way, exist to deal with those who manifestly harm, damage or destroy the individual citizens within the community. They identify the wrongdoer and determine what should be done to him or her. The courts lay down fines, imprisonment or even sometimes the penalty of death.

These duties are taken for granted in the Christian tradition of political thinking, and they are also commonplace outside it. There is, however, a negative aspect to coercive power. We find in Scripture that the perversion or abuse of duties such as we have described is roundly condemned. A legitimate use of the State's first, external function of protection is implicit in the words of the prophet Amos about unprincipled warfare, in which the necessity of the State to defend its own citizens from external attack is used illegitimately in barbaric ways. In the first two books of Amos, chapters 1 and 2, we find Amos looking beyond Israel and pronouncing doom over other nations. "The Lord roars from Zion and thunders from Jerusalem" (Amos 1:2), against Damascus, the cities of the Philistines, Gaza, Tyre, Edom and others.

Amos gives the grounds of his prophecy: the list is a sombre one. The nations are to be held to account for their abuse of power. Damascus, "the foreign city most influential in the politics of the entire region",[11] is condemned for her barbaric, savage punishment of the Gileadites who resisted their invasion by Damascus. Gaza has plied the inhuman trade of selling captives as slaves. Edom has matched Gaza in the taking of slaves, and the Ammon has matched Damascus in brutality in war. The list goes on: treachery in regard to international obligations, merciless hatred of other countries continuing far beyond anything that might have been justified, cruel imperialistic demands, the desecration of the dead. It is a catalogue of abuses in the sphere of social policy, and the nations are being judged for those abuses.

[11.] David Allan Hubbard, *Joel and Amos* (IVP, 1989), p.131.

Amos's denunciation makes straightforward assumptions about the moral insights of communities, far beyond the light of immediate revealed truth such as existed in Israel through God's law. Inhumanity and cruelty are seen as penetrating that first function of the State, the external duty to protect the community. In condemning the abuse, Amos affirms the value of the duty.

We find throughout the prophets many suggestions that within the community – in other nations and even within Israel itself – the legitimate power given to the State for policing and judging justly and equitably has similarly been abused. Often they suggest that there is injustice in the legal system and that money has changed hands.

Towards the end of Solomon's reign, along with the king's own spiritual and moral decline, came a decline in the quality of the measures he adopted. For example, he adopted forced labour as a deliberate social policy (1 Kings. 9:15–22):

> *All the people left from the Ammonites, Hittites, Perizzites, Hivites and Jebusites (these people were not Israelites), that is, their descendants remaining in the land, whom the Israelites could not exterminate – these Solomon conscripted for his slave labour force, as it is to this day (9:20–21).*

It was an act of exploitation towards strangers in the land – the extent to which Israelites were pressed into service also is not clear – and it was part of Solomon's social policy. It was not a temporary aberration of social justice, for Solomon's son Rehoboam continued and intensified the policy:

> *The king answered the people harshly . . . . "My father made your yoke heavy; I will make it even*

heavier. My father scourged you with whips; I will scourge you with scorpions" (1 Kings. 12:13–14).

And Scripture condemns coercive power within the community, used as Solomon used it towards the end of his reign and as Rehoboam used it after him.

*

What biblical insights can Christians contribute to the discussion about equality and compassion?

As Christians considering the proper function of the state, we contribute first *the Christian view of human nature*. Human beings are created in the image of God but are now fallen; their total moral physical and spiritual health has been overtaken by an acute infection. This is a very simple fact, yet often our legislators forget it. Humanity was created in harmony with God, but men and women are now divided within themselves and are hostile to God, their Creator. The first human beings were created naturally obedient; the commands of God (such as they were) fitted them completely, and they happily obeyed. Now we find ourselves to be transgressors. The image of God, in which we were made at the beginning, is defaced. The mould from which we all come has been cracked. Unless we are influenced otherwise, our natural tendency is to prefer wrong choices to right ones, disorder to order, exploiting our neighbours to fulfilling their needs. The apostle Paul expressed his frustration over this central cast of human nature:

I do not understand what I do. For what I want to do I do not do, but what I hate I do. And if I do what I do not want to do, I agree that the law is good. As it is, it is no longer I myself who do it,

*but it is sin living in me. I know that nothing good
lives in me, that is, in my sinful nature (Romans
7:15–18).*

This understanding is central to a Christian view
of society. That is why Jesus himself used those
notable words against the Pharisees, when he warned
them that their constant stress on external purity had
eliminated from their minds the far more important
fact that evil comes from within a man: "What comes
out of a man is what defiles a man":

*For from within, out of the heart of man, come
evil thoughts, fornication, theft, murder, adultery,
coveting, wickedness, deceit, licentiousness, envy,
slander, pride, foolishness, all these evil things come
from within and they defile a man (Mark 7:20–23).*

That is our first, very pertinent contribution when
we are thinking about the State. Man is fallen, and
therefore controls are essential.

The second insight is *a realistic view of human
society and its needs*. Because both good and evil flow
from the heart when human beings live together, two
things are needful. The first is space for choice. Men
and women need to be able to make personal choices.
This is the only way their gifts and potentialities
can blossom for the benefit of their fellow human
beings. But the second, correlative, need is that as
well as being creative, we must also have reins and
curbs.

Freedom and order must be held in balance; the
possibility of growth, and also the possibility of
protection from evils around us and sometimes evils
within us. In theological terms, the art of government
has always been to discover how to balance legislating
for the image (the good in mankind) and legislating
for the infection (original sin). Achieving some sort of

balance or synthesis between providing the freedom for men and women to grow to be themselves, yet at the same time ensuring that sin within us is reined and curbed – this is the challenge to the state.

The third insight is the biblical perception of *the awful nature of anarchy*. The Bible suggests that there is no more frightening situation than that when law and order break down completely and every man is "free to do what is right in his own eyes" (Judges 21:25). It is an invitation for the bully to take over. It is what happens in the playground when the prefects or the staff disappear. When the law of the strongest prevails, then we are indeed in a most terrible plight.

This again has to be balanced against another principle. The fourth Christian insight is *the fact that there is no greater potential for large-scale evil than despotism*.

How often a nation invests one man or a small élite with absolute power, expecting thereby to be preserved through a difficult period; and how often the experiment has resulted in lasting harm and hurt! The lesson of prewar Germany is all too easily forgotten. I can remember a time when it was still fashionable to joke about the Nazis. We used to say, "Well, at least Hitler made the trains run on time". And there was indeed economic and social renewal under Hitler; for example, Germany built its autobahns before the USA had freeways or Britain had motorways. And in the early stages of the Nazi regime, after the decadence of the twenties and the Weimar Republic, there was much that made the German people heave sighs of relief and welcome somebody at last who seemed to have a grip on things. But Adolf Hitler's grip was too tight. It was unrestrained by any other political or moral process, and soon the devastating results were only too obvious.

The same is evident in many Marxist states today, and also in the Islamic revival states. This has something to do with the concept of God in Islam, which has a fierce, unitarian, concentrated energy to it. The Islamic concept of Allah has a hyper-masculinity which Christians cannot share. Despotism is evident, too, in some South American states. Very often it is the dictator and his family who are vested with absolute power.

The Old Testament shows us something of this danger even within Israel. Immediately after Solomon's death, the kingdom crumbled. Why? Because under Solomon, a very significant change had taken place. Until David's time, the king certainly embodied the law, but he was not above it. When the king is spoken of in the Psalms, the image is of somebody who is the source and authority, yet is always under God and his laws. Monarchy is something that is allowed rather than commanded. In the book of Deuteronomy, when kingship is defined, it is made clear that the aim of monarchy must not be to become a great military power. The king must immerse himself in the law of God:

> *When he takes the throne of his kingdom, he is to write for himself on a scroll a copy of this law, taken from that of the priests, who are Levites. It is to be with him, and he is to read it all the days of his life so that he may learn to revere the Lord his God and follow carefully all the words of this law and these decrees and not consider himself better than his brothers and turn from the law to the right or to the left (Deuteronomy 17:18–20).*

Sadly, by the time that Solomon ended his reign this pattern of biblical, godly kingship was lost in

Israel (1 Kings. 10, 11). Solomon had become like other Near-Eastern potentates of his day. Like them, he accumulated wealth and splendour, built up his armies and weaponry, regarded himself as above the law, and did exactly what he wanted.

The tragic story of Solomon's decline and death is recorded in the Bible. It starkly spells out, relatively early in the history of civilization, the dangers of despotism.

*

Having described four fully Christian insights into the workings of society, we must now go on to ask how those insights relate to Western liberal democracy. And the answer is that they affect us very profoundly, because the roots of our institutions and of our very existence were fashioned under such insights.

Only one group in the wide family of nations has managed to avoid the twin evils of anarchy and despotism, and keep a fairly even keel. They are the most thoroughly Christianized countries, where the early achievement of mass literacy and the availability of the Bible came together to add to the wider social ferment of the fifteenth, sixteenth and seventeenth centuries. They are, in fact, the countries of Europe and North America, and more particularly the Protestant countries: Britain, the Netherlands, Switzerland, Scandinavia, Canada and the United States of America. In these countries there has been a wider exposure to biblical truth, to biblical preaching and to the printed word. By those means the culture has been cleansed and invigorated, even in its political thinking. These nations have achieved a balance; not a static condition but a stable, creative tension between the need for order and the need for freedom. Sometimes the balance has been an uneasy one, but it always has been there.

In a negative sense, this was rooted partly in the fear of anarchy and partly in the fear of despotism.

*

Christian writers on the principles behind our Western liberal democracy have often begun by discussing respect for individuals. That respect is implied by the fact that we regularly consult each adult individual on the question "Who would you like to run the country?" The ballot box is recognized as a compliment, implying respect for every individual in the country. A General Election implies that people count and that the people as a whole matter; that every adult citizen ought to be consulted. Here again is a value which ultimately goes back to the Gospel itself. Christianity rejects all the juggernaut theories of history and society. They tend to crush the individual, giving him no possibility of changing or altering things, or encouraging him towards channelling his thinking into the political process.

Earlier centuries acknowledged the superior importance of kings, emperors, popes, bishops and other rulers, giving them the last say – sometimes the only say – in the political process. The modern form of tyranny, however, accords greater value to the whole historical process, which some sort of omniscient party apparatus (under the genial guidance of Karl Marx, Lenin and others) must interpret for us. It is a different kind of juggernaut, but it is a juggernaut just as certainly as that of the all-powerful emperors of earlier ages. Yet Europe and North America are not governed by that kind of power. The reason is, surely, that we have been taught for centuries that man was made in God's image. We have acknowledged that every person will answer to God one day, even the rulers. And we are called to love our neighbours as ourselves.

These doctrines have acted as a healthy leaven, causing men to respect each other. Respect means listening to others, and giving them a part in the ordering of society.

Thus, the right to vote is a profoundly Christian privilege. G.K. Chesterton once wrote, "Universal suffrage is an attempt to get at the opinion of those who would be too modest to offer it". The echo of the New Testament is plain.

The other emphasis that comes with this respect for the individual is a parallel truth – our realistic assessment of human nature. Writing in his biography of Mandell Creighton, Lord Acton remarked: "Power tends to corrupt and absolute power corrupts absolutely." That is a Christian insight.

The remedy is to ensure that power is spread as widely as possible, in order to avoid this danger. As C.S. Lewis remarked, the "true ground" of democracy is that:

> Fallen men [are] so wicked that not one of them can be trusted with any irresponsible power over his fellows.[12].

Note that Lewis talks of "irresponsible" power. We all need to be held in check at times. Nevertheless, here we have something which is profoundly Christian – one of the basic insights which have led to our Western liberal democracy.

[12.] C.S. Lewis, "Membership", in *Transposition and Other Essays* (Geoffrey Bles, 1949), p.39, and in *Fernseed and Elephants* (Fount Paperbacks, 1975)), p.11.

*

We must turn now to certain twentieth-century emphases that have created problems in the democracies belonging to our own European culture.

We try to work for justice and mercy. We all want a community which is merciful and we all want a community which is just. But in that quest there are slogans and priorities which have presented us with difficulties, particularly in the last fifty years. I want to identify three of them, and consider them from a Christian viewpoint.

*

First, there is *the humanistic or atheistic erosion of the roots of law*. We can trace the beginning of this in the very early years of modern democracy. As Christians, we believe that the roots of all goodness and truth and the unchanging principles that ought to underlie any political system have been revealed once for all. But in the last years of the eighteenth century, when modern political democratic thinking was being forged and democratic political systems were emerging, we see departures from clear, revealed Christian principles. The Ten Commandments, for example, were quietly jettisoned in favour of something rather more vague. Interestingly, nature and nature's God are not yet excised from all these early declarations. The French Declaration and its preamble, dated 3rd September 1791, states:

> *The representatives of the French people constituted in national assembly, considering that it is igno-rance, forgetfulness and scorn of human rights which are the sole causes of public evils and the*

> corruption of governments, are resolved to expose
> in a solemn declaration the natural, inalienable and
> sacred rights of man, and that this declaration (con-
> stantly present to all members of the body politic)
> shall remind them ceaselessly of their rights and their
> duties, so that the acts of the legislative power and
> those of the Executive power, open to be compared at
> any instance with the goal of every proper political
> institution, may be the more respected, and so that
> the claims of the citizens, founded henceforth on
> simple and incontestable principles, shall always
> turn to the maintenance of the Constitution and
> the happiness of all. Consequently, the national
> assembly recognizes and declares in the presence
> of and under the auspices of the Supreme Being,
> the following rights of man and citizens.

Nature and nature's God may sound sketchily drawn, but the words are there. The reason, I believe, is that though there was clearly a process of secularization beginning, undoubtedly with the weight of the Enlightenment behind it, yet there remained an instinctive persuasion that these rights needed a transcendental foundation. Only a justification above and beyond any particular human community would suffice; rights must be rooted in God himself.

So here is an example of radical, revolutionary, anti-clerical French leaders dragging in the Supreme Being – imagining, perhaps, a sort of invisible chairman. Nevertheless, here also is an admission of the need for a transcendental grounding of human laws. And any declaration of human rights without this grounding (as many intelligent men in the eighteenth century who were not Christians realized) becomes the purely arbitrary creation of those who are in a position to create it. It becomes what Marx said it has always been: simply an expression of the interests of the ruling class, whoever they might be.

Yet a statement such as this suggests that we ought to look at the roots of good law; at binding obligations, which somehow come from above us. Inescapable imperatives press in upon all of us, rulers and ruled. That is what the phrases of the Declaration suggest. And Christians will agree with them.

But if this secularization process is taken to its logical conclusion and the concept of God goes up and up, even further away from theism to deism, and then from deism out of the window . . . what then? If God is not the Celestial Mechanic, but just disappears from sight and is totally removed from any kind of involvement with the world, then we are left with practical humanism or atheism. In those systems of belief (or unbelief) there are no grounds for any kind of categorical morality which should be expressed in the law. The moral law becomes essentially a decree that I issue to myself, or a standard which any community chooses quite arbitrarily to impose upon itself. Under those conditions there is no proper foundation for law. Good law in society will wither. As Christians, one of our responsibilities is to remind our fellow citizens of this fact.

Humanism and atheism produce this profound rootlessness of human law and confuse men about the function of the State. Why should the State do one thing rather than another? This intractable problem – for a Godless society – has been summarily but powerfully highlighted by Francis Schaeffer in *A Christian Manifesto*,[13] which, despite some limitations, is required reading for Christians.

[13.] Francis Schaeffer, *A Christian Manifesto, passim.*

*

The second twentieth-century problem is the whole matter of *compassion*. What is the place of the quest for compassion in social policy? In Britain immediately after the war the right and proper appeal to compassion touched the Christian heart as well as the wider community. Post-war Britain saw the emergence of the Welfare State by common consent; Sir William Beveridge (1879–1963) was the architect of the plans for comprehensive "Social Security" and a National Health Service.

The words "Welfare State" are still used with a positive weighting in Britain as a complimentary term. The principle is admirable – social provision for the least fortunate. The state should provide for those who for no fault of their own are suddenly "dropped on the scrap heap", those who find it difficult to continue to subsist in any kind of meaningful style through lack of food, shelter and basic care. The disadvantaged, those who are born with handicap, those who suffer accident in any way, those who through illness are incapacitated, those who are old and can no longer earn money – all these should be supported by the citizens who are active, earning and able to be more self-sufficient. Ideally, this provision should extend from the cradle to the grave. So we have provided a National Health Service, National Insurance and state pensions, unemployment pay and so on. In America, there are equivalent programmes.[14]

The arguments to justify this kind of provision are two-fold. Firstly, the moral instinct of any humane society is to wish to care for those who are less

[14.] For example Medicare, a provision of the American Social Welfare program, providing for older people.

fortunate. That is a profoundly Christian instinct. The second consideration is a contingent fact about our society; that those of us who are citizens of modern Western nations live in affluent societies. We are able, by common consent, to impose a degree of taxation on those who are earning, so as to enable us to make large-scale social provision for the inadequate.

In pursuing these policies of compassion, we have found ourselves up against a whole series of problems. Firstly, *the fact that the help that we give is obligatory*. It comes via taxes which are imposed, and some people (though not many) object to this. It may be that behind the modern propositions for less taxation we see some rooted objection of principle to helping anyone by decree. There are those who will say that they certainly wish to help the unfortunate, but they do not like to be obliged to do so by the government's imposition of heavy taxes.

The next problem is *the creation of bureaucracy to administer* which is often resented as oppressive. Bureaucracy has increased rapidly and extensively since the Second World War, and part of this is certainly due to ambitious programmes of social assistance for those who have fallen upon hard times for one reason or another. Yet we all know that bureaucracy tends to mushroom, and is typically inefficient and typically costly. This has caused great heart-searching on both sides of the Atlantic during the last twenty years; at the time of writing, both the USA and Britain have governments dedicated to cutting down on bureaucracy.

The next problem associated with social policy and directed towards compassion is *the fact that it creates dependency*. In almost all the fields of social inadequacy, the system creates groups of people who will not in fact learn to help themselves. From the point of receiving centralized help, they lose the incentive to stand upon their own two feet or even the desire to make long term plans to do so. This is a fact of sinful nature.

Perhaps all compassionate social policies have to live with this flaw. In Britain, social service scroungers do exist, and they have been a good source of political rhetoric since Mrs Thatcher came to power. However, nobody knows exactly how much the British Social Services are abused. The existence of abuse does create tension at the little glass window where the bureaucrat confronts the inadequate and the needy. Many cases of genuine injustice stem from interviews at the little window, because the bureaucrat has his book of rules to apply, and he knows that there are scroungers. He tends to become a kind of inquisitor, just because claims have to be sifted, documented and confirmed. As a result some citizens are unjustly treated by the very bureaucrats who are put there to exercise compassionate policies.

Finally, and perhaps most serious of all for the Christian, *the Welfare State can easily generate a social climate in which real compassion disappears*. If you think that you have already given enough (perhaps too much!) in taxation to help the inadequate, you will not feel encouraged to put your hand into your pocket for more when an individual case comes directly to you. You will tend to say "no" to a small local group requesting assistance. You will be tempted to say "I have already helped. Why should I give them yet more? Let them go to the government." Thus compassionate provision by centralized social policy can actually sap the genuine compassion of individuals in the community.

Christians conclude that the principle of taxation itself must be right. It is there in Scripture (Matthew

22:15–22; Romans 13:7). Taxes are needed for defence purposes and for the police, the courts, and good order purposes. These are essential functions of the state, as we have shown. But how much should we tax for "compassionate" provisions, those less tangible purposes of social welfare and social benefits? Certain items are less controversial than others, such as the preservation of the national heritage in the shape of important monuments, buildings, national parks and so on. Parks are also very important, because Britain is a smaller country; preservation of unspoiled natural landscape has been a major concern of ecological groups and has also been part of government policy. Again, the provision of roads is a national responsibility; here too we need overall central planning, direction and funding. Other public services such as water, sewage and electricity make legitimate claims.

But soon we enter other areas and services which are more problematic. What of schools, universities, railways, refuse disposal, air transport, medical care, pensions – can we draw a Christian line at any point? The New Testament certainly encourages us to pay our taxes, to render unto Caesar that which is Caesar's, but first-century provision in the Roman Empire was not linked with compassionate welfare-type policies, so it can be argued that the taxation texts in the New Testament are not actually very much help to us.

There is no single solution for all societies. The level of taxation needs very careful assessment in every individual community, and Christians must be involved in establishing that level. When does taxation become so burdensome as to be hostile to compassion, and therefore harmful? When is it so low that it becomes impossible for the community to provide even the most rudimentary safety net for those who need help and can get it from nowhere else? The answers will depend on national resources, the level of national prosperity, and national needs. Active voluntary benevolence is a very important element in the life of any country, for a number of reasons. So even on pragmatic grounds, there is a reason for avoiding heavy taxation: if we go on passing resources to central government to provide a multitude of compassionate services, then taxation becomes over-heavy and voluntary benevolence is undercut; and the idea of neighbour-love goes sour in many minds.

In Britain we have tried to achieve the balance of a hybrid system. In many fields Christians are behind the voluntary caring work, and the government will say, "We have allocated money to help this needy class of people, but as you are already working in the field we do not need to assign government personnel to the task. We will let you carry on. You are a reputable group, you present accounts at the end of the year; so here are the resources to enable you to continue doing the work, and even to extend it." Over the centuries many Christians have benefited from such policies.

It is a sad thing, therefore, when the State has to take over functions that previously the churches and individual Christians have discharged out of the love of Christ. All too often, the original motivation fades away.

I can think of one very sad example. The probation service has its roots in the early nineteenth century when prosperous Christians who had the time to do it went into the courts, and stood by young delinquents and young offenders and helped them. Their aim was not primarily to avoid manifest injustice, but to make a personal contact in order to give personal, spiritual help to the accused. They would then be able to visit the offender in prison and perhaps offer advice on such matters as rehabilitation and finding employment. It was a totally voluntary, church-based work. Today's probation service is different. Probation officers are given a lengthy training, but the firm moral Christian content of the Victorian pioneers is absent. In the sociologist's jargon, the probation service has become professionalized and totally secularized.

I believe that the emergence of the professional caring services in the place of voluntary Christian activity has brought some serious losses as well as some gains. An active Christian concern for public morality could cope with far more of those problems if it were widely shared. That is why I believe that a Church that is preaching the Gospel and thereby, under God, creating compassionate individuals who take real initiatives independent of government, will make it more difficult to make the case for statutory, centralized tax-supported initiatives in compassion-ate social policies. This in turn reduces taxation and avoids the emergence of costly bureaucracies.

It is worth recalling that Emile Brunner, the great Swiss theologian, maintained that the State should not be in the business of compassion at all. Justice and not compassion, he argued, should be the sole guide for the State. It is an important distinction, as well as a useful emphasis which accords with New Testament teaching. It will appeal to many, especially when they become aware that state benevolence is running into the sand.

*

We turn now to the quest for equality, and we soon

discover Christian roots again, in the respect due to every man because, though fallen, he is made in the image of God. Since we *are* all fallen, just as we are all made in the image of God, are we all equal? From the divine standpoint, the answer is in no doubt. We are all made in God's image, and we are all guilty sinners in need of salvation.

One non-controversial implication of this is the need for equality before the law. It is generally agreed that the courts should be open to all. But what of wealth, or of property or of power? Should we constantly redistribute these "goods"?

Here we face one of the dilemmas of democracy. If we provide a free society, equality of opportunity will tend to generate certain subsequent inequality. In other words, we find that we have given people the opportunity to become unequal. Yet equality of opportunities seems a right and proper thing to have, since it allows people to grow in freedom and to develop their talents, and very often to use them for the common good. Christians can only welcome this. However, if such a policy means baptizing all aspects of an unrestrained capitalist economy such as flourished in late eighteenth-and early nineteenth-century England, Christians must have serious doubts. Such freedom soon breeds exploitation of man by man – unless there are moral and spiritual controls.

As society becomes more secular we see a return to the harsher features of early nineteenth-century England. The ethic of many people today seems to be: "Maximize consumption"; there are no moral criteria at all. Apparently it does not matter what the product is, or how useful it is. That is one aspect of an unrestrained capitalist economy, especially in its later stages; and it is a state of affairs that Christians must seriously question.

For example, advertising disfigures many European and American cities. Ubiquitous advertising is an invasion of our thought life which we cannot avoid in the streets and on commercial television. Some of the finest brains in the land, some of the highest-paid men, are engaged in this industry; and their efforts are devoted to trying, for example, to sell more soap powder. What does that say about our values and our culture? Brashness, heartlessness and self-indulgence predominate. People are still exploiting each other, in these and many other ways.

If the State exists to protect the vulnerable, then it can be argued that there should be a little more intervention in some spheres than there has previously been. In Britain, the Monopolies and Mergers Commission and the Advertising Standards Authority are part of the answer. But each measure to intervene has to be strong, with meaningful powers. For example, the Advertising Authority, like the Press Council, is a voluntary body established by its own industry, and therefore exists by consensus rather than statutory power. Similarly, the government warning on the side of cigarette packets is of very little use. And all governments are scared to do anything about the biggest addictive item of all, and the most destructive – alcohol.

How can we secure a Christian approach to equality? The Old Testament certainly adjusted property inequalities. The Jubilee system (Leviticus 25) was one way of doing so, and tackled some extreme cases. There are similarly serious judgements upon those who "lay field to field" (Isaiah 5:8), in other words, the growing enterprise in which one man controls more and more so that other people become merely tenants, or exist as serfs without rights.

However, in its warnings against massive accumulations of wealth, the Bible does stop just short of saying that wealth *itself* is an evil. Let me emphasize the words "just short". Riches can be used to God's glory, and many Christians have used them so. But there are many biblical passages, such as those presented by Ron Sider,[15] that warn strongly about the dangers of accumulating money: for example, wealth creates a tremendous risk and a temptation, as Jesus warned his first disciples (Mark 10:25); the typical persecutor of Christ's people is a rich man (James 2:6–7,5:1–5).

On the political level, private property creates a problem for every community. Is it the State's duty to curb the accumulation of private property when it gets to a certain point? If so, when is that point reached? When is further wealth unhealthy and clearly against the interests of the majority? Are there some things which the State should allow no one person to possess? Christian thinking can establish broad limits, but no more. Yet a few guidelines on equality can be indicated, and we must try to make them clear.

*

Firstly, we need to remember that *equality is not the same as justice*. Sometimes Christians use the words as if they meant the same thing but they do not. Justice means each man receiving what is due to him – praise or blame, reward or punishment. These are individual, not identical. There is no suggestion in the Bible that each man deserves exactly the same in every respect. Justice demands a genuinely moral

[15.] Ron Sider, *Rich Christians in an Age of Hunger* (Hodder & Stoughton, 1979).

perception of what men deserve. The brave, the industrious, and the bearer of great responsibility in society rightly tend to be recompensed generously. Bare equality, as the sole and overriding ideal, would simply mean that we should carve everything up and give everybody the same. This could be seen as a rather crude social morality at the start of a community's life, but it should not be confused with justice. Justice means discrimination of what a person deserves.

Next, *complete social equality is illusory*. It is a will-o'-the-wisp. All societies which have pursued it earnestly find they end up with a terrible inequality of power, since in order to get equality the State has to take complete power to make it work. You have to have Controllers with a capital "C", who will decree what each person is allowed in every sphere. It needs a totalitarian society to impose equality. Marxist theory points towards a final egalitarian society, but Solzhenitsyn's description of the means adopted to achieve it in communist countries is a sobering warning.

Thirdly, *a Christian has a vested interest in diversity*. He worships a God who is three in one. Humanity exists in two sexes, man and woman. We look around us and see in the world an infinite number of species, fish and birds and plants and flowers. In the non-living world the simplest example is immensely persuasive – no two snowflakes are the same. There is a wonderful diversity in the world that God has made; the world of the enthusiastic egalitarian, by comparison, is not only inhuman but very drab.

Fourthly, *egalitarianism as an overriding social ideal prepares the way for one old-fashioned sin in particular: envy*. If our attitude to our neighbour is to assert that "I am as good as you", then we will tend to make the further assertion, "I am entitled to what you have, and I am grieved that you possess advantages, material goods, or other benefits when I lack them." So envy is produced, and the result is that our appreciation of what God has given to us as unique individuals is distorted. And so is our appreciation of our neighbour, who soon becomes simply a target of resentment and cupidity.

It is a short step from individual relationship poisoned by envy, to national resentment which shows itself in international actions that carry immense consequences.

But if we accept that equality, in the sense in which it has often been used, is a delusion, then compassion, service and obedience all become meaningful concepts again. And human beings can strive to protect the vulnerable and defenceless in their society, recognizing that not all have equal access to law, or care, or even (in the case of the unborn child) to recognition as a meaningful human being in the first place. These are issues we will be considering in the next chapter.

IV

Public Policy and
the Value of Human Life

In the previous chapter we examined some of the dangers and pitfalls to which contemporary framers of social policy have all too often succumbed.

I want now to look more positively at two areas which seem to me to emerge as positive values so sharply from the Bible and from human experience that we can regard them as legitimate aims for Christian people – and we can even draw along with us non-Christians too, though their basis is different, and their actions lack a foundation.

Firstly, I want to address myself to a very specific issue, the value of human life. I want to see first what a secularist *can* say; secondly, what a Christian *must* affirm; thirdly, under what circumstances society may take human life legitimately; and fourthly, where public policy has gone astray and where we are running risks.

What can the secularist say?

I delivered the lectures on which this book is based having come straight from the US Senate hearings on the Human Life Amendment, under their chairman, Senator John East.

The Hearings demonstrated to me that on many issues Christians will find themselves aligned with secular co-belligerents.[16] One woman present, for example, represented Libertarians for Life, a totally secular organization. She was carrying Bernard Nathanson's book *Aborting America*;[17] this is a key book, showing how a humanist Jewish surgeon can completely change his view after running the largest abortion clinic in America. Nathanson now holds a pro-life position.

Yet I would maintain that the secularist logically has no ground on which to base his belief about the inviolability of human life and the preciousness of the individual, except for what we may call "prudential considerations". Such considerations (for example, the thief taking precautions in case he is caught) do extend to this area of life; for example, any encroachment upon the protection of life is potentially a threat to the aged, handicapped or those born with congenital disease or having disease diagnosed in the womb. The secularist, therefore, can legitimately appeal to prudential considerations; but I believe they provide only limited help, and do not comprise a logically sound basis, nor can they inspire the kind of drive and conviction that the Christian possesses.

The words of a leading atheist biologist typify humanist concepts of what life is all about: "genes fighting for survival". But if that is all there is to human existence – "Godless evolution", if you want

[16.] I have supplied here the useful term "co-belligerent" – used by Francis Schaeffer in similar discussions, notably in his *Christian Manifesto* from which Raymond Johnston has quoted earlier.
[17.] Bernard N. Nathanson with Richard N. Ostling, *Aborting America* (Life Cycle Books, USA, 1979).

a more emotive phrase – then of course, human destruction along the way might even be welcome in many cases. After all, it is the fittest that deserve to survive; and if I am stronger, then the interests of the whole race might be served by my killing you, if you happen to be genetically inferior or likely to bequeath a lower quality of human life to the next generation.

Many people alive today have lived through a time when that thinking was enshrined in a political system by the Nazis. The only person who had a complete right to survival, they maintained, was the perfect Nordic individual. All others had a much lesser right – particularly if they were Jews, handicapped, elderly or could not contribute to the war effort.

The result was the extermination camps.

I hope you have read at least one book about the Nazi regime and what it actually did. I find surprising ignorance among Christians about exactly what went on. I hope you know the figures involved: six million Jews, for example, systematically exterminated because they were, according to the racist Nazi theory, subhuman. The theory is sometimes called social Darwinism. Strangely enough, it was invented in the more Christian atmosphere of Victorian England by Herbert Spencer, who was a friend of Darwin; but it produced evil fruit.

Hitler's racial theories, when examined in black and white, are of course nonsense. They are not even grounded in good biology. Nevertheless, if there is no God and there is no transcendental sanction for our distinctions between good and evil; if life is simply a struggle, a conflict between warring factions, and if that is the only rule – then perhaps a purifying of the race, permitting only the survival of fitter individuals, is ultimately the only thing that can justify one person surviving and the other not. If the law of the jungle enriches the genetic pool, why should we hold it back?

It seems to me that secularism and atheism are bankrupt on these grounds, so far as care for one's neighbour is concerned. This road leads to an existential wilderness, without significance for the individual's life or for history. So why should you bother?

Happily, through God's common grace and the remnants of the image of God in man even after the fall, the universal human conscience knows rather more. And it will testify instinctively against atrocities that devalue the worth of human life, as indeed Nazi Germany was universally, and instinctively, condemned. In Christian or non-Christian, there is a moral awareness that says: "This is monstrous, this is inhuman; and we cannot go that way." That is why the golden rule which Jesus gave us, that we should do to others as we wish them to do to us, finds an echo in all cultures. Many, if not all, civilizations have something of that in them.

C.S. Lewis ends his *Abolition of Man* with a section with an appendix, entitled "Illustrations of the Tao".[18] In it, he assembles a large collection of statements and testimonies from a variety of world sources, from many civilizations and various historical periods, and from all ages. For example, you find that the statement in ancient Egyptian literature, from the Book of the Dead, that "I have not slain men" is a self-justification before the gods; so there exists in that ancient literature the conviction that the gods cannot tolerate murder. Similarly, an Old Norse legend describes a vision of the after-life: "I saw murderers in the Norse hell."

The European mind, thank God, was sickened at

18. C.S. Lewis, *The Abolition of Man*, pp.49–59.

the gas chambers of Nazi Germany. One has to add that it was profoundly disturbed at Hiroshima and Dresden, where the West itself towards the end of the war engaged in blanket bombing to a degree which many people still feel was unacceptable. We must admit that we are not totally guiltless. Today we wrestle with the problem of mindless terrorism, about which our media, who report it so well, find themselves unable to make much of a moral judgement.

Is not that interesting? Of course, it is the secular climate; the reporter's attitude is that his job is not to make judgements but to give news. But what must the Christian affirm, in the face of widespread assaults on human value and life itself? The Bible is absolutely clear. I have reached my own conclusions about its teaching on these issues only during the last ten years, since they first surfaced and confronted Christians. But the only way to reach any conclusions at all is to do so with our Bibles in our hands, seeking to rediscover basic biblical insights.

So we begin with the Bible's massive, positive affirmation that *God made man in his own image*, so that man is in a very special way an image of his divine creator. What could be more sacred therefore and more dignified, than knowing that you are made in God's image – and so is every man, woman and child upon this earth?

Yet, some will argue, that image has been ruined by the fall. But that leads to the second biblical truth: *incarnation restores our belief and clarifies it again*. God saw fallen human nature. He decided to redeem a people for himself, and he did it by coming in their flesh as a human being. So it is impossible to dismiss appeals to the fact that man is the image-bearer of God, on the grounds that the fall has happened.

After the fall God still took our nature; so that Christ is the likeness of God (2 Corinthians 4:4), reflects the glory of God and bears the stamp of his nature (Hebrews 1), and is the image of the invisible God (Colossians 1:15).

These passages speak of a *man*, Jesus of Nazareth. And incredible as it may seem, there is the image of God in man, perfect again.

Thirdly, for this reason *the archetypal transgression was, and is, murder*. Genesis 4 reveals the first anti-social sin, the first conflict; it reveals how Cain killed Abel. It was wilful, malicious homicide. It is an example of how depraved human nature can be, of what sin makes one man do to another, even within the family.

Therefore, very early on in Scripture – long before Moses – *the death penalty for murder was solemnly proclaimed by God*. "Whoever sheds the blood of man, by man shall his blood be shed" (Genesis 9:6). Clearly, in the beginning of history, God is saying to mankind that there is one reason which justifies the solemn taking of human life: that is, murder.

In the same chapter the original creation mandate is repeated: mankind is to multiply on the face of the earth, and to have dominion over all other creatures; but at the same time, when the image of God is so desecrated by this particular crime, there is only one proper penalty for it. Only one penalty satisfies the terrible injustice, and that is the death penalty. It is a solemn and tragic underlining of the value of individual human life. So when we do get to Moses, in Exodus 20, we find murder forbidden. One commandment is devoted to that, and then in Exodus 21 we have the judicial penalty reaffirmed with the death penalty for the offence. And we are thereby introduced to some basic affirmations about the value of human life, the seriousness of murder, and the solemn penalty God attached to it from the beginning.

*

But we need to set this biblical truth in a wider context, and ask ourselves this third question: under what circumstances may the deliberate taking of life become legitimate?

Christian theologians seem to be agreed on the following cases.

Self-defence

There is an interesting passage in Exodus 22, covering the situation when somebody kills a criminal who is in the act of breaking into his home. It is not clear what the thief's intentions are towards the resident's person. He may just be looking for valuables, or he may have murderous intentions. The killing, in Exodus 22 therefore, is not regarded as involving blood guilt. However, it is not made clear whether this is a ruling that covers all defence of self. But Christian theologians have developed a logical case from it to cover defence of self against a clearly murderous attack. In such a situation you may not intend to kill your attacker. You may only intend to disable or maim him, or in some other way to hold him up until the police arrive or until you can get other help or until you can escape. But if you *do* kill him, we are not dealing with a murder, with deliberate, malicious homicide. We are dealing with killing in self-defence, which is a different matter.

If that is true – and it is a commonplace of moral theology – then the same can, and should, apply to communal self-defence, such as is necessary where a whole community needs to defend itself against murderous attack, invasion from another nation.

It must be said that there is a respected pacifist tradition in the Christian Church, which has existed since very early in Christian history. There are those who have said that there is never any justification in a Christian taking up arms at all. I value this testimony, and I think that we need to hear it. We need to hold a dialogue with our Mennonite brothers and sisters and others who look at conflict in this way. Yet, though I do not wish to devalue their position, I believe that theirs is a case that cannot be sustained categorically from Scripture; that the right of nations and communities to defend themselves must involve use of arms, and therefore warfare.

Charles Hodge, the American theologian, freely conceded the appalling nature of war.

> *It is conceded that war is one of the most dreadful evils that can be inflicted on a people, that it involves the destruction of property and life, that it demoralizes both the victors and the vanquished, that it visits thousands of non-competents of poverty, widowhood and orphanage, and that it tends to arrest the progress of society in everything that is good and desirable. It is also conceded that the vast majority of wars which have desolated the world have been unjustifiable in the sight of God and man.*[19]

But Hodge continues, and I would agree with him, that having granted all that (and we must grant all that if we are to take warfare seriously as a ghastly evil), nevertheless in a fallen world we have to consider two things. Self-defence is the right of nations as well as

[19.] Charles Hodge, in his third volume of Systematic Theology.

individuals; and the State is here and is bound to protect the life, the property and the peaceful going about of their business of the citizens it represents.

War commanded by God

On some occasions, God has *commanded* warfare. He may not do so today in the way he did to Israel in biblical times, but nevertheless warfare cannot totally be ruled out if on some occasions he sanctions it.

In the New Testament John the Baptist in Luke 3 is asked to advise the soldiers of his day, who were asking, "What shall we do?" If the answer had been "Repent and believe, and lay down your arms", John could have said it, and they would have done it; because this was a decisive intervention in history. A revelation was in progress, and John was a mighty character of strength and conviction – but he did not say it. He simply said that they were to rob no one by violence, to make no false accusation, and to be content with their wages. The men repented, and went back to their military service, with a higher ethical standard for their profession.

Jesus, you may remember, in Matthew 8 was confronted by a centurion whose faith and lifestyle amazed him, in so far as the Son of God could be amazed. He was amazed by the godliness of this man who came asking for healing. He commended his faith, but never told him that he must go back and, if he were truly to follow Christ, lay down his weapons and look for another kind of job. The same thing happened to Peter, who was sent by the Holy Spirit to Cornelius, a man of the Italian cohort who was waiting for the Gospel. He waited for the Gospel, he heard the Gospel and he believed; the Holy Spirit fell upon him, he was baptized and he received the teaching of Peter, the leader of the Apostles. Yet he was never told to leave the army.

These are some of the considerations that must be taken into account when we think about the New Testament attitude to war. It is not prohibited, and indeed no historic church has actually outlawed war. The Archbishop of Canterbury put the case in a nutshell when he said, "I fought in the last war myself: and believe that although war is evil and does terrible things to those involved, sometimes it is necessary, in order to restrain and defeat even greater evil."[20] The Second World War was an example of a just war. That does not justify all that we did in that war, but it was essentially a just war. And it is possible to say that and also to concede, with Charles Hodge, that the majority of the wars that have desolated the world have been unjustifiable. But there are such things as just wars; and a nation has the right of communal self-defence.

That right, however, is not unrestrained. The only consideration that would make the production of nuclear weapons fully justifiable would be a public commitment never to be the first to press the button. NATO today has not made that commitment; its weaponry is not only ready for "first-strike" use, much of it is the kind of weaponry that only makes sense in a first-strike capacity.

Yet though it remains an ideal only, the principle of eschewing the first strike does offer a theoretical justification for possession of nuclear weapons. If Western Europe and the United States are to preserve their own way of life, rooted in individual freedom and justice and concern for all against what is manifestly tyrannical and inhuman, then there is only one way to come to the disarmament negotiating table.

[20.] Said when preaching at the Church of the Epiphany, Los Angeles.

82

And that is to ensure that one's own stockpile is as large as the others.

If that is so, then negotiation will be possible, because the retaliatory threat is a real one and and has to be taken into account if a nation is planning a first strike.

But a unilaterally diminished stockpile, viewed in the context of increasing stockpiles in other nations, will mean that proposals will not be taken seriously – there is no longer an effective deterrent. At the same time, the possibility of a conventional aggression against Europe and perhaps against Britain, increases dramatically.

Consequently the military leadership of NATO and America is committed to a strong nuclear deterrent. I thank God for it. May it soon be completed by a deep moral commitment never to be the first to press the nuclear button. That would make clear that the emphasis of the West is the defence of its own countries. While first strike remains a possibility, and we maintain the weaponry with which to achieve it, there remains the disturbing possibility that some day the West might consider it justified to take advantage of a superior level of nuclear armament.

*

We have seen that Scripture affirms the right of individual self-defence and that of communal self-defence. Now, thirdly, we come to the death penalty, the due legal penalty for crime.

The crux of the case lies in what crimes may be held to merit the death penalty. The fact that the rights of civil authority extend to the right to take life is made clear in Romans 13. Civil authority "bears the sword", which can only mean the right of capital punishment.

However, in the Old Testament the death penalty is applied to more than murder (defined as a capital crime, as we have already seen, from the very earliest times). Entire classes of crimes attracted the death penalty in Israel, and these we must now consider.

We begin with the *homicide* group of crimes: this includes, obviously, murder, and also child sacrifice. The keeping of an ox that has killed human beings is regarded as a capital crime, for it is demonstrably a menace to the lives of others. False witness on a capital charge is also included, understandably: to send somebody to the electric chair or to the gallows on a false charge is tantamount to taking his life unjustifiably, and so that too must attract the death penalty.

Next there is the *family* group of capital crimes. It includes kidnapping a child and insulting or injuring one's parents. It also includes incest.

Sexual offences include adultery, bestiality, sodomy, premarital fornication, fornication by a priest's daughter and the rape of a betrothed woman. This group includes a wide-ranging variety of offences.

Finally, there is the group of *religious* offences. This includes sorcery and witchcraft, false prophecy leading to idolatry, idolatrous sacrifice, sabbath-breaking, and usurping the proper office or functions of an Aaronic priest.

*

In the Old Testament, all these attract the death penalty. Today we may see the legitimacy of taking life in self-defence or in warfare, but what about all these other situations?

I would personally wish to make murder a special case, for it seems to stand out in Scripture from all these others: though obviously it can only be used if one has a judicial process which is reliable and stable, and which, if any doubt whatsoever exists, will not impose the penalty. But what about all the other offences?

I believe that the possibility must be retained that the State may take life for other crimes than murder. I believe that this is a negotiable matter, one which depends on the strength of values in society, the degree to which it is necessary to deter criminal behaviour, and the degree of horror that is felt against certain crimes in society. All these things need to be taken into consideration before it can be decided what crimes, apart from murder, should attract the death penalty; and if those crimes are judged deserving of capital punishment, then the due process of law, the rules of evidence, the objectivity of the judicial process and so on must all be given due weight.

*

It could be argued that none of the non-homicidal cases above ought to attract the death penalty: that God was fashioning Israel in a way that he had never fashioned any other nation. So, it could be argued, those crimes were decreed as incurring the death penalty *in Israel* – but God has said nothing about what other societies since must do. He could have decreed that these crimes should attract the death penalty; but he has never said anything about what other societies since must do. That is a perfectly tenable position. Nevertheless, some crimes other than murder seem to me to be possible candidates for capital punishment.

Take, for example, treason and terrorism. The crime of "high treason" has been acknowledged in Britain since the eleventh and twelfth centuries. Terrorism is a modern phenomenon; the successful terrorist is usually a threat to many lives, not just to one. It could even be argued that the unsuccessful terrorist who fails in his act of terror should still suffer the death penalty, because terrorists are people who have abandoned all respect for human lives, including innocent civilians'.

However, another factor in the matter is that we have available to us today a range of penal sanctions which Israel did not have. We have fines, prison and various restitution procedures, some of which are proving very effective. In America, for example, research into rehabilitation testifies to some instances of real personal change, quite apart from instances of religious conversion', where young delinquents guilty of assault, stealing and similar crimes have been ordered by the courts to go and work for the person or persons whom they have wronged. And there is some genuine rehabilitation of offenders taking place.

Christians involved in ministries such as those of Prison Christian Fellowship in Britain and Charles Colson and his ministry in America, who are thinking creatively about such matters, are working in an area where there are really exciting developments to be explored.

Where have policy and Christian morality quietly parted company?

There can surely be no more crucial question for citizens than that which asks under what conditions human life can be taken legitimately in the community. Here, surely, public opinion and public legislation must take an urgent interest.

The first issue I want to discuss is *abortion*, the destruction of a human being at some point prior to natural birth.

Please do not use "termination of pregnancy" as a synonym for "abortion". The two are not the same. Every gynaecologist, Christian or not, should allow the possibility of terminating a pregnancy and saving the child. The ghastliness of abortion lies in the fact that it is practised with the deliberate intent of destroying the child.

The question that is raised is: is it, or is it not, murder? It is deliberate. It ends an innocent life that cannot possibly have committed a breach of the law. It is enacted upon a defenceless human being. And it is enacted without any due process of law. And I believe that the following points indicate that abortion is, in the sight of God (and so it should be in the eyes of mankind) clearly tantamount to murder.

It is true that the Bible never mentions deliberate induced abortion, so there is no explicit biblical ruling on the matter. Nevertheless, by the end of the first century, one of the Christian ethical distinctives was already that Christians did not practise abortion. The *Didache*, an early manual of moral teaching and guide to conduct, was probably written before some of the latest epistles in the New Testament: it is against abortion. A prohibition against abortion was among the severe canons of the Council of Elvira (c. A.D.306).

By the end of the second century, the influence of Christianity had brought Roman law to forbid abortion, long before the conversion of Constantine and the Christianizing of the Roman Empire. Long before that, under the Emperor Severus, Roman law forbade abortion. This was the influence of Christianity, over a hundred and fifty years.

The medical profession has never wavered over the last two thousand years – until our own lifetime. This was very powerfully expressed by Dr Caroline Gurster in the Senate hearing I mentioned earlier.[21] She quotes the Oath formulated by Hippocrates, one of the earliest Greek doctors, in 400 B.C. He was going against the tide, she points out, but his position was this: if we are going to have a medical profession, if we are going to have specialists in any sense, then they must have the highest ethical standards. And doctors will have to say "No" to some of the things that are tolerated in society.

The Hippocratic Oath begins with a commitment by the would-be doctor to teach students honestly, to regard the student-teacher relationship as being like a parent-child relationship. The oath goes on to bind the medical student to teach his children so that there will be a tradition of medical teaching without charge; to follow the method of treatment that according to his ability and judgement will be to the benefit of his patients; and to abstain from whatever is harmful and mischievous. And then come these words:

I will give no deadly medicine to anyone if asked, nor suggest any such counsel. Furthermore I will not give to a woman any instrument to procure an abortion.

Well, we know what has happened to the medical profession in our own lifetime, but that was the ethic of the medical profession from 400 B.C. onwards. The Arab doctors accepted it, the Christian doctors accepted it. In Britain, for centuries a pregnant woman convicted of a capital offence could not be hanged – because she was bearing another life; you would be

[21.] Raymond Johnston, delivering the lecture on which this section is based, had come directly from the hearing.

killing two persons rather than one, which was so manifestly unjust that the execution could not be allowed to take place. By 1910 every state in America had clear anti-abortion laws.

By the end of 1970, eighteen states allowed abortion in "exceptional circumstances", though the imprecise wording of the law permitted a multiplicity of reasons. More states followed, and in 1973, the historic 1973 *Roe v. Wade* ruling by the Supreme Court established the right to abort, and overturned all remaining US anti-abortion legislation.[22] In Britain, the 1967 Abortion Act opened the doors to abortion on wider grounds than the safety of the mother or other "exceptional" circumstances.

At the time of printing this book, it is being suggested[23] that *Roe v. Wade* may be overruled in the near future; and in Britain, the pressure group within Parliament seeking to reverse the 1967 Act has achieved a high media profile; though the measures proposed have been defeated in the House of Commons, the campaign has had some effect on government policy. Nevertheless, these remain for the present partial or hypothetical victories. We live, in the meantime, in the wake of a huge revolution in attitudes towards abortion in the past thirty-five years. And the key question raised is this: is the unborn child (for me as a Christian and equally as a member of the human race) entitled to my brotherly, neighbourly protection? Is it entitled to the same protection I would seek to give to a person I saw being attacked in the street? Is the unborn child my neighbour – or not?

I think there are some considerations that help us to answer this question.

[22.] Cf. Richard Winter, *Choose Life* (Marshall Pickering, 1988), p.34.
[23.] E.g. in "The Battle over Abortion", *Time* (17 July 1989), p.32.

Firstly, *ignorance points only one way*. If our answer is "I do not know", or if I hold that there must be a point between conception and childbirth when the child becomes worthy of my protection but that I do not know when that point is – in either of these cases of ignorance, it must follow that we have to protect the child from the moment of conception onwards, because you could not accept ignorance as a morally valid defence in any comparable case.

Consider the case of a man lying in the street, having been run over or knocked down. You would not say, "I wonder if he is dead or not? I do not know. So I'll leave him, I won't try to save his life, I won't even call the ambulance." On the contrary, you would say that *because* you did not know, you would go straight to that man's aid and help him as much as you could. Why? Because he could be alive; it is possible that his life may be saved. If I say that I do not know when the unborn child becomes a person, or when it becomes the proper subject of my protection as a fellow citizen, then the moral consequence must be that I begin my protection of that child from the moment of conception, simply because I do not know, and because otherwise I could be making a terrible mistake.

Secondly, *human life is genetically complete at conception*. Everything that made you physically and materially what you are (apart from the intervention of God the Holy Spirit at conversion) was present at your conception. The colour of your eyes, the colour of your hair, the height you were to grow to, the kind of hormonal balance you have – everything about you was present at conception. All you needed from conception onwards was food, warmth, space and protection. You were all there at your conception.

Admittedly, at the beginning you did not look

much like a human being, though we now know that after a few weeks in the womb, you did. In any case, the fact that a person does not look like a human being is not an argument for not protecting him. If you are a doctor called to a major disaster, you do not discuss whether somebody looks enough like a human being before being treated. You just give the treatment. Why should an unborn child be treated in precisely the opposite way?

Thirdly, no criterion of "full humanity" will justify induced abortion. *There is no point at which you can say that you are fully human.* Ask a number of people at what stage after birth you become fully human, and you find all sorts of cut-off points suggested. Does it come when you can speak? When you can walk? When you can relate to people as a mature adult? If the latter, many of us have still not reached full humanity!

Fourthly, *human life is a continuum in which birth is only one event*. What is natural birth today could have been induced childbirth yesterday, had the mother been given a birth-inducing drug. Indeed, the baby born by natural birth today could have been delivered by caesarian section a month ago.

If this is true, then natural childbirth cannot be taken as a landmark. There was somebody there before, somebody who could have been brought into the world as a human baby earlier. Nor is size a criterion. Some babies born by natural childbirth are so tiny that they are smaller than many babies born a month or two earlier. All these are sliding scales; and there is no cut-off point at all between conception and natural birth, such that a Christian can say, "Here is the point before which you can abort, and after which you have a real person [or a full human being, or whatever phrase may be used]

– that may not be aborted."

Fifthly, *the teaching of Scripture*. When we look to the Bible for guidance on this subject we find that the biblical writers are conscious of God's hand upon them long before birth. Think of the birth stories that go back long before conception: how many individuals – such as Samuel, Samson, Jacob and Esau and Jeremiah – were either called by God, or were spoken of in advance, long before the moment of their natural birth?

This does not make the case unanswerable, but it is an important factor. It seems that in Christian revelation, there is a view of the person as being in some sense "there", capable of being discussed as a person, from conception onwards.

But what *does*, in my opinion, conclusively resolve the issue is the use of the Greek word *brephos* in Luke 1:41. It means "the child". "The child leaped in her womb" – it is the same word as is used for a child *after* birth. And, more than leaping in her womb, the child apparently was filled with the Holy Spirit. Elizabeth spoke of the pregnant Mary as the "mother of my Lord".

This brings us therefore to the Christian affirmation of the incarnation, which leaves us no room for escape at all. If you are an orthodox, well-taught Christian who is asked, "When did God become man?", you will respond with the Apostles' Creed: "conceived by the Holy Ghost, born of the Virgin Mary". That is when he became man.

But if that is true, then manhood begins at conception. And if the proper man – that is, Jesus – began his earthly existence as a human being at conception, then so do all human beings. It is inescapable. For example, it is a main plank in the Roman Catholic and Anglo-Catholic platforms. That is why they are so clear when you talk to them about abortion. It is something I have had to learn. I owe it to some of my friends on that end of the ecclesiastical scale. Some of us do not work so easily with the doctrine of the incarnation as we do with the doctrine of the redemption.

But the incarnation argument is perfectly clear. If Jesus became man at conception, and was really man so that the whole of his manhood developed as ours does (and that is what is involved in saying that he was a real human being), then to know that his human life began at conception must mean that ours does too.

The consequences for public policy are momentous. Those debating in the congressional hearings were doing something which, whether they knew it or not, was profoundly Christian when they proposed that human life before birth should be entitled to adequate protection under the law. I believe that the implications of the incarnation for the unborn child are such that every faithful Christian should be a supporter, in some sense or other, of the pro-life movement. I know that many people, and many of my readers, are doing splendid work in this area.

Of course, it will mean that we must be committed to the enactment of legislation to reverse the terrible 1967 Abortion Act, and in America the terrible 1973 Supreme Court decision *Roe v. Wade*, and *Doe v. Bolton*, when Chief Justice Blackmun ruled that meaningful humanhood did not begin before birth. That is the most terrible statement, in the light of what I said earlier.

*

And so we have the strongest possible grounds: medically, philosophically on the grounds of human rights, and scripturally on the grounds of the limitations put on the taking of human life and the incarnation, for joining with all others who want to see this anti-life legislation reversed.

I would like to quote from some of the literature of the British group, Lawyers for the Defence of the Unborn. It is not a religious group, and it has no religious affiliation. It has over eight hundred members, all of whom are practising lawyers, barristers or solicitors. At one of their conferences, a professor of law – Professor Laysock of Exeter University – addressed them:

> Our 1967 Act reversed one of the basic assumptions of our system of law: that the law serves to protect the life and bodily integrity of the individual. It is a licence to kill.

Equality is overturned by this legislation, and there is no equal treatment of born and unborn. Nor is there equal treatment of father and mother, for in Britain the father has no right whatsoever to make any representation to the law in respect of the child he has begotten. Some years ago in Britain the Paten case was a major news story. A father tried to stop his wife having an abortion. He said that it was his child, and he had equal right. Legal commentators are divided on whether he presented his case in the best way, but certainly the arguments he placed before the court could not stop the child being destroyed. Professor Laysock said later that this was a denial of the due process of law. The unborn was neither represented nor heard; moreover, for the purpose of the operation he was not the subject but the object of the law. Not being the subject of the law, he was not a bearer of rights and duties, and so was not a party to the process to determine his existence or otherwise, but was merely an object to it. That could not be due process of law.

An appalling comparison comes to mind. In wartime Germany a very simple device called the Nuremburg Laws was invented in Germany. Under them, certain categories of persons were dehumanized; and being deprived of their legal personality, they were merely an object, not a subject of the law. In such reasoning, to kill a Jewish or Polish inmate of a camp was not a crime. To degrade them and to experiment upon their bodies was not a crime. It was merely a job to be done. That is how the Nazi law worked.

I thank God for the work of Francis Schaeffer and Everett Koop, in particular their splendid film *Whatever Happened to the Human Race?*, which challenges lethargic Protestant Christians to face this issue.

*

In conclusion, let us briefly consider the other methods of taking life that are ruled out.

Infanticide. The killing of children after birth is clearly the next logical step after the medical profession has become accustomed to the idea of abortion. What logical reason is there for protecting a child *after* birth, when he or she can legally be destroyed at any time in the first seven months of pregnancy (and in America, right up to birth)?

Destruction of the human child after birth is unlawful under British law. Yet it is happening, ostensibly on the grounds of compassion – towards the parents who would have to look after a handicapped child, or even towards the child himself, on the argument that "It is better for him not to live".

But let him argue his own case! In *Whatever Happened to the Human Race?*, several severely handicapped children appear whose lives have been saved by Dr Koop. If you ask these seven- or eight-year-olds whether they are enjoying life, they say that they certainly are, and that they are very glad they were not done away with.

Or let a lawyer, at least, speak for them. At the present time no case has come before the British courts in which their point of view has been heard. Everything is done behind closed doors, by doctor's decree: "Sedate the child." If you sedate the child it will not cry. When it does not cry, the nurses – who are instructed to feed on demand – do not know it is hungry. And so the child is killed, by decrees issued by certain doctors. It is reminiscent of Hitler's policy: "Only the perfect shall survive." If you had blue eyes and fair hair, if you were an authentic Nordic man or woman, then you were entitled to survive. But if you were physically or mentally imperfect, or a Jew, or a burden to the State because you were old and in an institution – then you had no legal rights and you were done away with.

Christianity says the opposite. The maimed, the deformed, the sick and the handicapped are those for whom Christians have characteristically cared. We are the people who started the hospital system in Western Europe, as well as many teaching institutions; we founded the monasteries that cared for travellers and wayfarers. We Christians took in the sick and the deformed. And it all came out of the Christian view of mankind. My ability to love God is not determined by the physical wholeness of my body. It was Herod who sent out a decree that all the babies should be killed.

Suicide. Christian moral theology has always treated

suicide as self-murder; but this is another area in which the British social climate has changed.

Charles Hodge thought suicide so serious that he believed that by definition it excluded later repentance. He concluded that because it excluded repentance and amendment of life, it excluded the soul from salvation. I would disagree with Hodge on this matter, but it shows the seriousness with which earlier theologians took that matter of suicide. (Even today, Roman Catholic theology denies the suicide burial in consecrated ground.) But in the second half of the twentieth century we have become so soft that we scarcely think of suicide as a sin – let alone a crime, which in English law it was until recently.

In G.K. Chesterton's *Orthodoxy* (1908), he speaks forcefully and brilliantly about suicide. He calls it "the sin":

> . . . *The refusal to take the oath of loyalty to life. The man who kills a man, kills a man, the man who kills himself, kills all men. As far as he is concerned he wipes out the world.*

A case can be made for taking suicide far more seriously than most of us do today.

It is worth adding that neither of the two suicides recorded in Scripture involves admirable people. Saul was the king who started well but ended miserably, by consulting a witch. The other was Judas Iscariot.

Euthanasia. Euthanasia is the causing, or assisting, of the immediate death of the elderly, the infirm, the incurably ill, those in pain and so on.

Few people would defend involuntary euthanasia against the will of the patient or person. And yet as soon as you condone voluntary euthanasia, some procedure is necessary to decide that it really *is* voluntary. That raises some very serious difficulties.

Does it depend on the person's spoken agreement? Must it be expressed once, or on more than one occasion? Must it be written down – and if so, how do you decide whether the person wrote when in his or her right mind? The questions go on and on.

English law regards voluntary euthanasia as the same as assisting suicide, which in England is a crime. I believe that this is right, and that voluntary euthanasia, even when the person maintains that the dead person asked to be put out of this life, is a very serious crime.

Some years ago, a Commission of the Church of England produced a report, *On Dying Well*. It examined this issue in great detail and concluded that there was no way of determining whether euthanasia was genuinely voluntary. It rejected the view that people have a right to determine the moment of their own death. This is, of course, the Christian testimony. In some mysterious way the Lord determined when I should come into this life, and I am to leave it to him to decide when I should to leave it. Perhaps it will be in pain. I hope it will not be with too much pain, and today the medical profession can ensure that. But if it is in pain, then I will stand with my Saviour who died in pain.

But he who is the Lord determines the time, and it is no business of mine to ask anybody else to put me out of this life. I do not have the right to do that. I resign myself into the hands of a merciful Creator. He gave life and he takes it away.

The attitude implied by euthanasia is very different. It takes the place of God by making the decision to end life. Euthanasia, as a doctor friend of mine puts it, is simply doctors killing patients. The doctor becomes an executioner instead of the caring, curing healing person.

Even when he cannot heal, he can – with modern drugs particularly – alleviate pain. I thank God for the hospice movement which is spreading very fast all over Britain, where people are getting together and providing a most loving, caring environment for patients who are terminally ill, particularly where they cannot be at home and where the hospitals have no room for them or have even given them up. Christians have been the major force in the hospice movement, and in hospices the residents see real Christian love in action.

In Britain, Dr Cicely Saunders – who is a Christian – is the main mover in this field. I am sure that there are similar people in America, and in other countries. And it is vital that Christian work grow in this area and provide this positive, caring service. For if we do not, just as if we do not involve ourselves in crisis pregnancy counselling, we are vulnerable to the accusation that we are simply adopting harshly negative attitudes without any commitment to care. We must care for the girl being pressured to have an abortion, and we must provide the necessary care facilities.[24] And similarly we must care for the elderly and terminally ill in such a way that there will be no need, demand or case for abortion or euthanasia at all.

*

I end this chapter by recording again, as a convinced Protestant, my thanks to God for the firm stand taken by my Roman Catholic brothers and sisters on these life matters. I thank God, too, for the book

[24.] In the original American lectures on which this book is based, Raymond Johnston spoke appreciatively of the USA organization Christian Action Council.

by Dr Bernard Nathanson, *Aborting America*, an up-to-the-minute book by a man who has changed his mind without changing his religion. It is a book to read and to encourage one's friends to read; it is the most powerful thing I have read outside Christian writing, from a man who, after performing hundreds of abortions in New York, has now changed his position.

Finally I thank God for Dr Koop and for Francis Schaeffer, whose film and book *Whatever Happened to the Human Race?* have stirred the Protestant world in a way in which it ought to have been stirred long ago.

V

Public Policy and Family Values

In the last chapter, we looked at some false trails, the consequence of a humanism that deprives individuals or communities of a moral map and compass. Atheism lacks an essential direction; it has no transcendental backing for morals and the law. We saw that both Britain and America have, comparatively recently, lost the Christian moral vision of the sacredness of life, and most particularly in respect of the most vulnerable of all human beings – the unborn child. Our hospitals have been changed into death chambers for the unborn, and our doctors are now toying with infanticide and euthanasia. This is a fundamental violation of the individual at the very heart of our human rights, the right to life itself.

Now I want to make one further, important, step. Public policy and social patterns of behaviour can protect an institution.

*

By "institution", I do not mean a building but a way or pattern of behaviour – in the sociologists' jargon: "normative roles". That is, the things that people learn as little packets of behaviour which have a sense of "ought-ness". For example, "This is how I ought to be, or to act"; or "This is the standard I ought to reach if I am behaving in that way, as a mother, father, civil servant, doctor, dentist, teacher, minister" or whatever it is.

Normative roles can be protected by the State. People can be given special legal rights on condition that they live up to their responsibilities and duties in particular roles; and these particular "institutions" very often guarantee – to give only a few examples – life, liberty, safety and the rule of law. For example, the State must be positively in favour of *truth*. This makes a society happier and more harmonious, and enables law to function. It must follow that some kinds of falsehood are penalized. Truth being sacred, we teach children to be honest. We may also have laws against untruthful advertising and untruthful accusations against individuals.

Again, the State must actively support the practice of *keeping promises*. This is an essential benefit of social living, and therefore laws exist to protect people who sign contracts and so on. We buttress contracts, covenants and undertakings with law, and subsequently with penalties if people break them. Therefore, the State has an interest in people being reliable, in human integrity.

The State is also in favour of *respect for the individual* and therefore it is entitled to control propaganda of hatred and violence – for example, the racial hatred we have seen in Britain in recent years. There are laws to control that, and also to control the spread of sheer malice and hatred in publications.

Courts, contracts, mutual respect; they are all part of normative patterns of behaviour. You can protect all of them by law – though it is the moral climate and the moral convictions of individuals that are the strongest guarantees of their continuance.

I give these examples to show that in many spheres, public policy cannot be neutral. In both Britain and America there is so much talk about neutrality, pluralism and similar concepts that you would think that the State cannot be committed to anything. But I have discussed here three spheres in which, most people would agree, the State must be positively in favour of certain patterns of behaviour.

It may be asked, what of freedom? Of course, it is one of the most sacred words. The State ought to be in favour of increasing freedom for the individual: freedom from arbitrary tyranny, certainly. But it certainly should not favour freedom from the rule of law, nor from the obligation to tell the truth or to honour solemn undertakings, nor from the duty to respect, for example, life, property and other people's reputation. The word "freedom" is already qualified by some of the basic institutions we have discussed. The State has endorsed liberty, but, as also accepted the need for liberty to have certain limitations.

There are other issues in which the State has a very powerful interest on behalf of the citizens to ensure that they are not ill-treated or exploited. For example, only certain institutions can qualify a man to practise medicine, and it is obvious why: because otherwise there would be unqualified doctors making havoc amongst the community.

Now, the State may not actually do the accrediting of doctors, but it will have a government department that scrutinizes the standards of medical institutions that hand out qualifications to doctors.

*

My proposition at the outset is that family values are

part of this normative framework. We may have to argue this today; and I think we do argue it with many of our friends and neighbours, and perhaps governmental representatives – that society has a positive interest in preserving and strengthening family ties. These are values to which both Britain and America have been committed and should continue to be committed. This inevitably means that although we begin with a presumption of freedom, a society such as ours is vulnerable to anybody who wishes to destroy the family – either his own or somebody else's, or perhaps the family pattern in general; and we must find some way of curbing anti-family propaganda and anti-family activity.

It may sound a bleak prospect, but we will come round to how we do it later. For the moment, let us examine what Christian family values are. What are the values that we as Christian people would recognize? I have discussed these in detail in my book *Who Needs the Family?*,[25] and I will outline them only briefly here, with some references to the earlier book.

There are five dimensions of marriage, and two of family and home: these make up the total, and from Genesis to Revelation they are the same.

(a) **Marriage is between a man and a woman**.
In Genesis 1:27–28 we read that God made man male and female. There in that first chapter he put man and wife on equal parity and commanded them jointly to rule the earth and to produce children. A deeper complementarity is hinted at in Genesis 2:18–25 where the narrative speaks symbolically of the making of Eve out of Adam, and we have the phrase used which is taken up in the New Testament referring to marriage, "one flesh". Genesis 2:24 in particular

25. O.R. Johnston, *Who Needs the Family?* (Hodder and Stoughton, 1979).

104

is quoted by our Lord in Matthew 19:4–6 where he speaks of the absolute primacy and centrality of the new relationship formed in marriage.[26]

(b) **Marriage is a public covenant privately sealed**. The two must go together; there has to be a public declaration, a public undertaking by two people, a man and a woman, and there is the private seal of sexual union.

(c) **A permanent loyalty is established**. In Romans 7, in a little parenthesis at the beginning of a chapter which deals with quite a different subject, Paul says that a man and a woman are pledged to one another for life, until one of them dies. After that they are free. That is one of the most clearcut statements in the Bible on this subject, and one that is often difficult for our contemporaries to accept.

> *It is sometimes argued by today's favourite media advisers that it is far better for young people not to enter any long-term commitment (i.e. marriage) until they have found out whether they can live happily together, including sexual experiment. But there are many considerations which suggest that this is not the way forward to a productive relationship for the two people concerned, and certainly not in the interests of the wider society.*[27]

(d) It is also **an exclusive loyalty**. In other words, all others are forsaken when that covenant is made. "This is a new primary loyalty, a new basic allegiance which overrides other allegiances."[28]

(e) It is normally **open to parenthood**. In other words, children are to be expected. They are also

[26.] Ibid., p.61.
[27.] Ibid., p.45.
[28.] Ibid., p.61.

welcomed; and though there are times, places and occasions where a couple are called upon not to have children, such cases are exceptions.

(f)   Within the family there is a **hierarchy**. The husband is the leader, the person who is the ultimate fount of discipline, authority and protection. In order to assume that role, he has to be prepared to sacrifice himself totally. That, in many cases, includes sacrificing his own maximum advancement, his own maximum income and other things. He has pledged himself to his wife and his family; and certain things, whether it be golf, or an extra ten per cent on his salary, or anything else, then start to take second place. Nevertheless, he is the ultimate fount of discipline and the leader in the family.

The wife, on the other hand, has particular care of the children above all in their younger years, and is specially charged with the making of the home. Homemaking, if you read Proverbs 31, is certainly not just concerned with cooking and mending and so on. It is sometimes alleged that in Old Testament Israel women were subjected and suppressed, and that the texts in the New Testament are simply a hang-over from the Old Testament. But the wife of Proverbs 31 even sold and bought fields, which is a far cry from oppression by the husband.[29]

(g)   The family in the New Testament does not simply consist of mother, father and children – the "nuclear family" – but it is to be **open to others**. This includes the support of relatives in difficulty or in need, or the elderly; and of course it is open in a wider sense of hospitality towards others, and perhaps sometimes to the Church itself. The family is a wider thing than just the Western nuclear family. All the

[29.] Raymond Johnston devotes two complete chapters in *Who Needs the Family?* to the respective roles of the mother and the father.

verses in the Old Testament that talk of homes being open to aliens, strangers and relatives are relevant here. Indeed, there comes a point where the spheres of family and Church become complementary:

> *Recent experiments in community living, some the result of the charismatic movement, some stemming from the "house church" ideal and others in more traditional settings, all point to a recognition of the need for regular wider human contact beyond the nuclear family, though containing it and feeding it at the same time. . . . Is not the Church called to reconstruct something akin to the older pre-industrial networks? Is not this the way to show love and appreciation for those without families . . .*[30]

The Christian family is called to extend the bounds of its own caring beyond the immediate close circle of parents and children.

*

That is the outline of the Christian family. And sadly, every aspect of it is open to perversion. It is a corruption that ultimately derives from satanic influences. Let me go through the aspects again.

Marriage is between a man and a woman

The first aspect rules out *child marriage*, which has been a common perversion in some parts of the world. Marriage is between a mature man and a woman who are capable of founding a home.

It also rules out *sexual relations between adults and children*. Parents and society must be protected, on the basis of Christian marriage, from premature

[30.] *Who Needs the Family?*, p.37.

commitment and experiment. That is why Britain has established a realistic age of consent, under which the law says a girl may not consent to give herself physically to a man. And that is a protection for her, because we believe that below a certain age she is simply not ready for the seal of a permanent commitment. Below a certain age, we are talking of exploitation, not consent.

It also rules out *homosexual unions*. Scripture makes it clear that the sexual act belongs between a man and a woman, in marriage only. Therefore any kind of pseudo-sexual union between two men, or any kind of similar stimulus between two women, perverts the divine will. The New Testament says that it is against the light of nature (Romans 1); it is against the standards of the kingdom (1 Corinthians 6); and it is against the standards of the law of God (1 Timothy 4). The weight of the New Testament is against homosexuality.

The New Testament is not condemnatory, however, of friendships – even between men or women of the same gender. As Christians, we must not rush to conclusions when we encounter people who do prefer the companionship of their own sex. It is a sad fact that in Britain today, two men or two women sharing the same flat do give rise to comments of this sort. I hope Christians would not jump to the conclusion that this is anything but moral, good friendship. Even if there were an element of mutual attraction between two men or two women, what Scripture is condemning, and clearly condemning, is a physical, genital relationship. And that means that no Christian church can in any way sanctify, bless or hallow any such a union.

The third relationship that is excluded by the biblical man–woman definition of marriage is *any kind of sexual relationship between men or women and animals*. Such relationships are still occasionally brought to light, and in some places it is even presented as entertainment, as Lord Longford found when he visited Denmark with his Commission in 1972. It is a grotesque overturning and perversion of the law of nature, which is briefly mentioned in Exodus 22:19 and Leviticus 20.

A public covenant privately sealed

The second aspect is rooted, as we have seen, in Genesis 2:24: "a man leaves his father and mother." There is the public act of setting up the new unit – "and he cleaves to his wife" – and there is the private seal in a sexual union.

Thereby several patterns of behaviour are ruled out automatically for Christians.

Firstly, *fornication* – casual sexual encounter between the unmarried with no form of covenant. The New Testament is very strongly against it. Almost all the lists of sins include fornication, because it was so common in the ancient world. It was a comparatively new thing to have a group or sect living and abstaining from any kind of pre-marital sexual activity. We will soon be back there both in Britain and America, if we are not there already. In such an environment the Church ought to shine out even more clearly than it has done in the past.

Secondly, *cohabitation*: living with somebody in a sexual relationship when not married. It is sometimes dignified by the term "trial marriage", but that is an expression that Christians must never use. Christians can only talk about marriage or non-marriage. There is either one or the other. If there is no covenant, there is no marriage: a man simply moving in with a woman or a woman moving in with a man does not create a marriage bond. According to Scripture we are with each other for ever, pledged exclusively and permanently – or we are not, in which case we are not married, and the sexual activity is wrong for Christians.

But if there is a pledge between a couple and a biblical marriage exists, then how apt are the Bible's words, "You rejoice in the wife of your youth". Though we have been negative about the perversions of marriage that exist, there is something deeply positive at the centre of the Bible's commands to husbands and wives.

Thirdly, *prostitution* is ruled out. That is, mercenary sex; sex for money. Prostitution separates the private seal from the public covenant, which of course is absent. There is only the exchange of money. In Proverbs 7, we find warnings against prostitutes and adultery far stronger than any warnings that might be written today to warn a young man against visiting prostitutes.

But we should remember that though this is something to which Christians must be opposed, and prostitution can form no part of Christian behaviour, nevertheless the prostitute has on occasion come into the kingdom of God ahead of more self-righteous people (Matthew 21:31). And it is interesting to note that where there have been revivals there has always been rescue work among the prostitutes, and some Christians have felt specially called to go to these people and help them.

Rape is worlds apart from public covenant and private seal. These are voluntary, and imply voluntary consent to a union. But rape is an act of violence that denies the beauty and responsiveness of the covenant by consent.

Sex for entertainment is also ruled out, whether on the stage or in front of the cameras. It violates the private nature of the seal, and makes sex into a spectator sport which God has never meant it to be. Many psychiatrists have pointed out that the very fact that it is public completely alters the relationship.

Some sophisticated people in Britain have argued that if one imagines the couple on stage to be man and wife, then it would be acceptable. They argue that this has undercut our position. But, of course, this would not change the situation at all. The nature of the act is changed completely, it is impossible to perform any kind of sexual act to order for other people without the whole private nature of it, as a loving response between two people, being completely altered. So sex acts for entertainment, sex shows, pornographic magazines and so on are ruled out.

Marriage is permanent

The intention of marriage in the framework of Christian theology is that of a life-long commitment. This excludes serial marriage, in which a person marries, becomes less committed to his or her partner, ends the marriage, remarries, and begins the whole process over again.

The Bible does not prohibit divorce. It says that there is a sad need on some occasions to make some provision for divorce. But, if divorce becomes too easy, too popular, socially sanctioned and regarded as an easy option, we end up with serial marriage. This is clearly against the framework of Christian belief and morals. Happily, English law will not yet allow a couple to sign a contract for a ten-year, five-year or even a one-year marriage. It is either marriage, or it is not. I understand that the same is true in America.

In a purely secular ceremony, the state insists that you promise yourselves to each other for good. Marriage only for a limited term would not be marriage, and it would not be recognized as such in law: it must be until death. The death of a partner, of course, does free the other partner.

Divorce must be seen by Christians as a tragic option under certain extreme circumstances. It must not be seen as anything else. The grounds must be very serious; the Bible does not make provision for anything lesser.

Significantly, the Bible does not say that anyone *has* to divorce his wife or her husband; it simply says that they may do so if necessary (cf. e.g. Matthew 19:8, Mark 10:2–11, Deuteronomy 24:1–4). There is no obligation. Therefore all the reconciling procedures and every possible strategy must be employed to attempt to persuade the partner desiring the divorce to try again. If it is happening in a Christian context, then of course it will be appropriate to pray about it and to get good counselling.

Many Christian partners have felt that though their husband or wife has gone off somewhere else or even married someone else, and, as far as they can see, has deserted them permanently, they are not free to remarry until the other partner dies (passages such as Romans 7:1–3 are often quoted in this context). I realize that others would feel that such a view is rather strong and rigid. But I respect those who hold it, and I think we need that reminder.

In the New Testament, adultery is mentioned as a possible ground for divorce (Matthew 19:9); another ground is desertion (cf. e.g. 1 Corinthians 7:10–15). But even that can be healed; even an adulterous partner can be forgiven and taken back. The Reformers taught that cruelty was another possible case, and one can see why; but it may be that it is a ground for separation rather than total divorce. In the Reformers' view, cruelty between married couples was such an evil thing, and so against the marriage covenant, that it effectively destroyed it. Not everyone would agree with that, and personally I would not come down on one side or the other.

All these issues come to an acute focus when a divorced person wishes to remarry in the lifetime of a former spouse. The Church of England is split down the middle as regards this at the moment, and has not yet decided what to do about it.[31] The problem is this. Who discerns whether a person who is divorced and who wants to remarry again in church, but whose former partner is still living, is a person who should be married again – as opposed to a divorced person who should not? The door cannot be made open to everyone, because that would result in serial marriage, and it would be wrong for the Church to promote it. So somebody has to decide that a case is exceptional: that the previous marriage is so totally finished that the Church would be right to permit remarriage. But who decides? And how does he know he is not being misled or deceived?

Divorce is permitted in Scripture. But we are still left with many problems.

Marriage is exclusive

The perversion of the exclusive bond of marriage is adultery. Adultery is ruled out for Christians. In Exodus 20:14, one of the Commandments rules it out completely.

[31.] At the time of printing (March 1990), measures to permit the ordination of divorced men in the Church of England have been passed by both Houses of Parliament and await Royal Assent, upon which the Church's canon to permit ordination may be promulgated.

However, to that must be added that Matthew 5:28, where lust is described as tantamount to adultery in the eyes of God. I hope that makes every reader – especially male readers – wince, as it does me. It means that we have to take ourselves to task almost daily in a sex-sodden society such as we have at the moment.

That is why Christians are campaigning for some curb on the public display of sexual activity, and pornography in general, because it is simply a way of stimulating lust. That is the purpose of adultery. And the way that our society has developed, and the way that pornography has been used as manipulation for commercial purposes, is one of the blights of our civilization.

One comment often made by visitors returning from the Soviet Union is that it was very pleasant to escape from all the mildly pornographic Western advertising magazines and so on. Of course, the cynic will tell you that as you go into the Soviet Union with a copy of *Playboy* you can sell it to the guards for a high price. But nevertheless I think it is a better society than ours from that particular point of view, because it does not constantly fuel lust.

Marriage is open to parenthood

Marriage is God's context for the arrival and care of children. Of course a Christian couple is not obliged to have the maximum number of children possible until the wife ceases to be fertile; there is no obligation for this at all. Nor does it mean that every act of sexual union between a man and a woman must be open to the possibility of conception. This is almost the Roman Catholic view, which does not seem to me to be a necessary deduction from Scripture.

What is, I think, ruled out is what I would call deliberate, planned unparenthood; the attitude that says, "Here we are, married; but there are going to be no children, and that's final" – that, it seems to me, is ruled out for Christians, except for very weighty reasons indeed, such as health reasons, or a particular calling, for instance in a pioneering missionary territory.

Marriage involves a hierarchy

On several occasions in the New Testament, a wonderful hierarchy is described. It begins with God the Father, then beneath God the Father is Jesus Christ the Son. As Christ obeys the Father, so the husband obeys Christ; and so beneath the husband is the wife, and beneath husband and wife there are the children. Father, Son, husband, wife and children. This is found more than once, but each "head", each person who has a position over another, at every level, has sacrificed for the one below. This is what saves this hierarchy from being domination.

The Father sent the Son. He emptied Heaven of his Son, and there are indications in the New Testament that it was a terrible sacrifice. Christ came and gave himself for the Church, and that was his sacrifice. In Ephesians 5, Paul likens it to the sacrifice the husband ought to be prepared to make for his wife. Similarly both parents sacrifice themselves for their children.

Those of you who are parents know that particularly during the first fifteen years of the children's lives, you sacrifice all sorts of things – which add up in the long run – to make a happy home and to bring them up properly. The sum total of the sacrifice is very great at every level.

We come to very delicate ground now. But it seems to me that the concept of hierarchy rules out certain perversions that are common in our day. It rules out, I believe, public sexual identity policies that say that there can and should be no difference on any grounds in any aspect of public or private life, that there should be no distinction made between men and women. But it seems to me that there are differences between men and women and between children, and that Christians are committed to such differences.

It also rules out something in a very practical area: patterns of employment which draw married women out of their home and away from their children. I am not saying that the State should ban such employment patterns, but I *am* saying that Christians should criticize very powerfully anything which makes it very attractive for married women with small children to leave the home permanently, and to hand over the care of the children to other people. That is not what the family is for, and it weakens the family decisively.

A possible model for social policy might even include financial incentives for women to stay at home and look after their children, to compensate them for loss of earnings, so that they will be able to be in the home and the child will be with its mother in the early years.

A further perversion of family hierarchy which we must watch out for, and which may come in by way of cultural and educational priorities and influences, is the tendency to set children against their parents. That is why so many Christian schools are springing up, particularly in America; manifestly parents are finding that schools are teaching values and practices that are so foreign, and against their own deepest convictions, that the response of parents is to say, "We will take our children away, and we will have something different". But it is the responsibility of all Christians to recognize cultural and educational influences which will set children against their parents, and do what they can to avoid them.

Marriage involves extended care

The last of the aspects I mentioned is extended care – the open Christian home. Under this heading comes the importance of caring for relatives, visitors and lonely neighbours.

Such caring is often undermined by subtle factors. For example, I think that some of us, in our keenness to talk about the nuclear family (that is, father, mother and children) have suggested that this is *all* there is. Certainly, many of the advertisements beamed into people's homes convey an image of the wife, beautifully dressed, producing a beautiful meal from the fridge or the oven, and father coming home from work; and the children are part of that image, which is one of luxury centred upon the father and mother. Such advertisements rarely include grandparents in the picture, nor single relatives. You do not often see other people invited into the home – or when that does happen, they are asked in merely to admire whatever it is that is being advertised.

*

These are the some of the things we must notice and hold out against. How then do we commend the biblical pattern of marriage and the family in secular terms?

We start with four huge advantages.

First, **clarity**. All the points I have raised, though the world does not like them and they sometimes sound old-fashioned, are at least clear. The world is very woolly and vague in its thinking, even when using slogans such as "equality". But the Bible is not vague at all; it is very clear.

Second, **democracy**. We live in a democracy, and people are open to persuasion about all these matters. And we should be far more often in print, far more often writing books and also far more often in discussion with people. We should be the moral salt, when family matters and morals are in question.

Third, **enquiry**. People are asking questions. I find that when I talk or am in a discussion about the family, people are more open than they were five years ago. Family breakdown is now so common and people are so shattered by it, either themselves or their neighbours or relatives, that they are saying, "We have let things get too far. And what is all this about the old-fashioned family? It seemed to work – what was it exactly?"

So after twenty years of sexual laxity and even anarchy, it seems to me that there is a turning of the tide and people are enquiring.

Fourth, **evidence**. The evidence is accumulating in our favour. Anti-family experiments always cause pain and disaster. A couple in America wrote a book called *Open Marriage*. They are now divorced.

We are not saying that all marriages made on a Christian basis are perfect, and we have to be careful not to suggest that. In the Christian Church there are many tragic marriage and family break-ups. What we are saying is that taken over all, historically and psychologically, the Christian pattern makes for stability and fulfilment in a way that we could well do

118

with today. The evidence is piling up that the other experiments lead to unhappiness.

*

With these four advantages in our favour, we then go on to remind our fellow citizens of six facts.

First, **there is a close connection between social progress and sexual restraint**. This is an interesting matter that I discuss in detail in *Who needs the family?* I rely on Unwin, whose work in *Sex and Culture*[32] has never been contradicted, though it is thirty years old. Unwin compared sixty or seventy different societies from all over the world, and he worked out indices for the degree of sexual restraint that there was in each of them. He also examined the rate of progress in the arts, sciences and technology, and economic prosperity. He discovered, time after time, that it was the society which had a clear code of sexual behaviour and buttressed the family with sexual restraints publicly applied that prospered.

Conversely, it was the more liberated, "permissive" society, where there were no such restraints, that tended to run into the ground and fail to achieve that level of development in arts, technology, science and so on. In a nutshell, Unwin's findings indicate that promiscuity spells social decadence.

Second, *there is no substitute for marriage*. Marriage is the source of personal sustenance, care and love. There is nothing more stabilizing than the mutual caring of a man and wife who are committed to each other permanently. It is stabilizing *because* of the commitment; each can trust the other, each said it to the other solemnly on a particular occasion, and both knew they meant it. And thereby they are given

[32.] Unwin, *Sex and Culture*, 1960.

the chance to relax, to rest their will and weight on that covenant.

Marriage is also good for personal fulfilment as you see yourself mirrored in another person, who tells you what you really look like to the outside world and does so in terms you have never heard before; and occasionally that hurts. As both partners communicate in this way, each begins to see what he or she really is, as they grow together.

There is also healing in marriage. You can tell your wife or your husband things about your past that you have never told anybody else. This is possible in the perfect stability of a marriage relationship. It is possible to open yourself up; and healing can take place. This is another commonplace for people who are happily married. Psychiatrists and psychologists are pointing this out all the time. Jack Dominian, a very fine Roman Catholic psychologist – an expert in marriage breakdown in the London area – has written movingly about the healing that comes in marriage and can only take place on the basis of that firm framework of the exclusive covenant for good. On that basis, you can really build a new life.

So fornication and all these other things do not deliver the goods. We must look our friends in the face and say: "Look – forget my religion for a moment. Only marriage can deliver certain goods. Nothing else will. You will never get to that point where they are to be found if you are sleeping around, either within or outside marriage. The goods can only be delivered on the basis of marriage as Christians understand it."

Third, **there is no substitute for home, parent care for the new member of our human community, the new child**. The Policy Studies Institute has published a very interesting document.[33] The Institute is a completely secular body, but the document mentions the churches and Christian standards, and is very relevant to our discussion. Marriage, it said, is an institution central to society. That is interesting, from a totally secular source! It is the only place where children can really be looked after, where they can be cared for and can grow. Putting it crudely, Mum and Dad are exactly what we need. Everything else is a poor replacement. Of course, this does not include the cruel dad or the soft mum without standards. But parents in general have a huge advantage. They brought the child into the world and created that child under God; and all the care and all the love are naturally there to be concentrated upon it.

The security that the child needs can also only be produced inside the marriage relationship. Everything else is a very poor replacement. It is a commonplace of child psychiatry that divorce damages children. When you tear a marriage apart, children are terribly hurt and damaged. Again, there is massive social evidence in the Policy Studies Unit report and many other publications.

Fourth, **specific damage results from abandoning Christian family values**. For example, consider just some of the perversions mentioned earlier. Anybody who is an expert in child abuse – and I have met experts on both sides of the Atlantic, particularly when the British legislation on child pornography was being passed – will confirm the awful link between child pornography and child abuse.

Again, what has the spread of homosexual behaviour done to Britain and America? As acceptance of homosexual sexual activity has spread – at least in

[33.] A.J. Brayshaw, *Public Policy and Family Life* (Discussion paper No.3: Policy Studies Institute, 1980).

121

private, and according to general public opinion – people have become more confused about right and wrong in this area. Certainly in Britain we have seen an increase in inherently unstable men, and a weakening of the model of masculinity that is transmitted to the next generation. I say this without wishing to belittle in any way those individuals who have this problem. But, as time has gone by, there has been a real question mark about what it is to be masculine. And that is important, because these public models are important.

There has been a huge increase in sexually transmitted diseases. Syphilis had been virtually wiped out in Britain until the homosexual upsurge of the last twenty years, and now far more syphilis is transmitted between homosexuals than between men and women.

Fifth, **prostitution represents a growing lobby**. There is great pressure in Britain to legalize prostitution – loveless sex for money. Those who urge this have powerful friends. The prostitutes lobby in both Houses of Parliament, and there has already been one attempt – and there will be others – to legalize prostitution. It was Christians in the last century who opposed the same suggestion, and we may have to fight again. But I believe that we can all tell our friends that such patterns of behaviour are so hostile to the stability of marriage and proper sexual relations that the law rightly frowns upon them.

For example, sexually explicit material on stage, on screen and in print increases the incidence of serious sex crimes. Comparative statistics between countries leave no room for doubt.

Finally, **lust promotes licentious behaviour and is a threat to womanhood**. This is something that comes as no surprise to Christians. It has been very interesting in recent years to see feminists marching through Soho, the most depraved part of London from the pornography point of view, under the slogan "Reclaim the Night". They have realized, albeit rather late in the day, that true respect for female dignity involves being anti-pornography. Though many Christians have grave reservations about feminists who fight with the police and shriek abuse, it is good to see them adding weight to this particular insight.

Another source of damage is the widespread promotion of contraception. I have already emphasized that marriage is the right place for parenthood, and that marriage should be open to parenthood. But the contraceptive revolution is undermining the whole idea of it.

Should we hand out contraceptives to all and sundry? And if not to all, then to whom? British, and I think American, statistics demonstrate that handing out contraceptives to anybody who wants them does not reduce either the abortion rate or illegitimate birth rate. It simply does not work; and it is important to know these figures, because so many people are saying that contraceptives should be handed out to anybody – even to teenagers without their parents' knowledge. They argue that this is the way to reduce the abortion rate and the number of illegitimate pregnancies. In fact it does neither. The more we hand them out, the higher these rates accelerate. British statistics show that, and it has been admitted by the Minister for Health in the House of Commons. But within a few days he was giving more money to the Family Planning Association, to continue with even more sex education of that particular type.

The cost to the community of family breakdown is astronomical, and surely there are many hard-headed elected representatives who will listen, if to nothing else, then at least to pounds and dollars. The Report on Public Policy and Family Life looked at the actual cost of marriage breakdown to the public purse, the treasury.

> *To the State the financial cost of broken marriages is high and has many ramifications, supplementary benefit to separated wives, divorced and single women with children.*

A breakdown of the costs involved follows: for example, the cost of the court cases, when adjudication is needed about who gets what and in particular who gets the children. The annual cost is in the region of £579,000,000. That is Britain's bill for one year for broken marriages. This must mean that there are implications for public policy. So we can respond, "Religion or no religion, please let us do everything we can to strengthen marriage".

*

I want to add a few words about pressure points in public policy.

In a democracy, there is public opinion. Why are we not using the media more to speak of God's loving provision of marriage and the family? Or of the misery of men and women when man rejects that provision? We should be saying it loud and clear at every possible opportunity. Not apologetically quoting texts, saying "But this, of course, is only for us Christians". We have done that for far too long, out of a misplaced pietism: "Our little enclave will believe these things and behave this way, but the rest of them can perish . . ." But are we really entitled to let our fellow citizens damage their lives in this way?

Statistics show that if you open the doors wide to every kind of perversion of God's patterns then the cost to the public purse will rocket. There is every kind of secular reason therefore for us to get out into the public opinion field and say, lovingly and sympathetically (but firmly), "This is a better way".

There are more people ready to listen to the Christian voice on these topics today than there were five years ago. It is also true that there are many today who face a bleak future because of the damage done to them; and we have to be sensitive, as we speak and write, to the fact that some of our listeners and readers will themselves have had abortions, or divorces, or separations, or other similar experiences.

It is not always easy to speak as powerfully and clearly as you would wish, while at the same time remembering that some of your audience may well need special sympathy. They are the debris of the Permissive Society, that its evil delusions about freedom and liberty, and its urging to go out and enjoy oneself, particularly sexually, have created.

Our tone of voice matters, we must be reasonable, compassionate, sometimes even humorous – but nevertheless we have got to be firm and clear. We must aim to change the whole climate of opinion in our society, so that changes in public policy become easy if not inevitable.

What legislation can achieve

I hope that the fact that we have developed a case in relatively leisurely fashion about the function of law has not left any readers feeling worried about the law's capabilities. Law cannot do everything – but it can do a great deal more than many of us think. You cannot make God's laws into man's laws, but you can enshrine principles and priorities.

Law does not make bad men good but it can guide the weak. It can make it difficult for evil to flourish, and that is useful. Law is negative, and it does curtail liberty – but only so that other things can grow. Some things will always need curtailing. You can have too much law, but we have to have order. If religion and morality are weak then sometimes the law must be strong, because there is nothing else that is a brake upon evil. It is true that law cannot control thoughts, but it can stop people injecting certain thoughts into the minds of the whole nation; it can project communications from abuse and corruption.

Neither can law make men religious. But it helps to create an atmosphere in which the Gospel can flourish and be preached. That is why the New Testament says that we must pray for our rulers. We pray for our rulers so that there may be peace and so that the work of the Gospel may continue.

These are some of the positive functions of law.

So what legislative steps can we suggest in the family sphere? I would propose eleven at least.

First, both Britain and America need **a legal definition of the family**. For example, I am in favour of the work being done by groups in America to produce appendages to any Bill providing federal funding for Planned Parenthood. I support the view that if you are going to have massive federal funds injected into an organization that is claiming to work for the family, then steps must be taken to ensure that the money goes to the family and not to other causes. And you do this by appending a definition of the family.

The definition must be crystal clear. It must affirm that a family is a social group of two or more members, related by the ties of blood (by common descent), or by marriage (which means men and women in permanent, exclusive commitment, publicly contracted) or by legal adoption. Those are the three ways in which members of a family are related, and there are no others. The law could furnish such a definition and give it the force of law.

Second, there is a case for **legal recognition, or some kind of legal and economic advantage, for married people as distinct from co-habiting couples**. I am sure that it is wrong and tragic for tax advantages to be available for two co-habiting people which are unavailable to a married couple: and that is the case in Britain. It must be changed.

Third, I believe there is a case for **a compulsory waiting period before marriage – say three or six months**. That would allow a couple time to have second thoughts if necessary, and to encourage them to save money to make a more stable basis for their marriage. It would also enhance the social recognition of marriage. The nation would be saying: "Here are two young people taking a serious step. Because we are going to rejoice with them when they do it, and because they will be watched over in this act by a state official at marriage – because this is recognized seriously, we are going to ask them to wait six months from coming to the registrar or whoever takes the details, until the wedding can legally take place". This possibility was suggested by the Public Policy and Family Life document that I mentioned earlier.

Fourth, there is a possibility that **divorce should be made more difficult**. Should there be a waiting period here, too? Where are the reconciliation procedures? Should we make them mandatory, compulsory? Should we say that nobody can have a divorce at law, unless there has been a serious attempt at reconciliation, unless the couple have seen certain agencies or talked with certain people? Should we insist that this is done before we grant a decree?

In this context, I think that the move towards "no fault" divorce – that is, divorce without any need to prove in the courts that either partner had committed anything wrong, but that the marriage had simply broken down – is a very sad one. Christians should be saying here that there must not only be a fault, but a very serious fault, by one or both parties, before a decree is granted.

Many will protest that the clock cannot be put back. But I wonder, is that true? The Bible does not say anything about not putting the clock back, and a secular proverb is not going to bind me. I believe that we should be prepared to look people in the face and say: "Yes, it does sound old-fashioned; but if we have good reason for doing it, let's say that we think the divorce laws are too lax – we need to tighten them up." And we do have good reason to do so.

Fifth: lust, though it is in the mind, is created deliberately by certain types of publication. So **we need a strong, clear anti-obscenity law**, which covers written material as well as pictorial material, stage performances, films and so on. There are problems of definition, and we wrestle in Britain with the consequences of a number of legal decisions of recent years. But we must not give up.

Sixth, **heavy penalties must be imposed for rape, seducing a minor, bestiality, incest and similar crimes**. This is important so that we can register in law, even if it is only a few cases each year, the seriousness with which we view this kind of perversion.

There is a problem here. If two people engage in an act of adultery, prostitution, or homosexual genital acts, which all happen in private, it is very difficult to get proof in courts of law even if you have relevant legislation. How do you prove it? They are adult and they consented. It seems to me that it is very difficult, if not impossible, to take these types of crime to court.

Having said that, where laws exist saying that such acts are criminal, I am not suggesting that they should be repealed simply because they are not applied, or no convictions result from cases brought under them. Jesus did not say that adultery was not wrong when they brought the woman taken in adultery to him; he simply said that there was going to be no punishment for that woman today. He did not say that they were to take away the law.

There is a case for laws that you never actually apply. Declaratory laws without penalties may be of use. A country may have laws that simply say: "This country is committed to this standard." And when somebody breaks those laws you do not take him to court or fine him. That kind of declaratory law is particularly useful in the sphere of family values. There is also a case for setting age limits for these patterns of behaviour – as we do for homosexuality in Britain, which is still unlawful for those under twenty-one years of age.

A very useful approach which we employ in Britain is to acknowledge that acts such as prostitution, adultery and homosexuality may be difficult or impossible to apprehend and penalize; but that those who associate with others to promote them is another matter entirely. So the law looks at people who print propaganda for these activities, who provide facilities, who advertise for them and recruit for them.

This is our practice towards prostitution; payment of money in exchange for sex is not itself a crime. But anything else, such as hiring premises for prostitution, taking a percentage from the earnings of a prostitute, advertising a brothel, or recruiting people to become prostitutes – all these are crimes.

Personally I think this is a real way forward which we would do well to consider in a number of these difficult areas.

Seventh, **we should consider controlling the advertising and sale of contraceptives**. Perhaps we should say, "Never to minors"; that it is a crime to offer, sell or distribute contraceptives to anybody below a certain age. The Christian position would be that they should only be sold to married people. I understand that this is so in the Republic of Ireland, where contraceptives are available in various ways but only to people who are married. At the very least, the health hazards of promiscuous sexual intercourse ought to be presented on every packet.

Eighth, we should consider whether to **refuse legal adoption to any but married couples**. Such a law would, for example, exclude two lesbians living together.

Ninth, should we **refuse artificial insemination in law, or make it illegal to artificially inseminate anybody except a woman with the sperm of her own husband**? That, I think, is the Christian view; any other act would be tantamount to adultery, albeit in a strange, mechanical way. I would like to see artificial insemination legally restricted to husband and wife.

Tenth, should we **outlaw certain materials in schools**? That is, material that promotes promiscuity, employs obscene language, trains children in the use of contraceptives when they are under age, ridicules religious beliefs, assists the spread of venereal disease, distributes information about homosexual intercourse, or contains similar information. It would be possible to draw up a statute that declared that certain types of material should never be used in schools.

Eleventh, and finally, we should consider **giving parents the right to inspect all materials for use in**

schools in sex education, to question their child's teacher about the sex education he or she is going to be given, and to withdraw their children from sex education if they do not agree with the values being promoted at that school. We very nearly had this passed by Parliament recently, and we shall return to it.[34]

Conclusion

The greatest preserver of family life is the Christian family. So when your pastor or teacher preaches these values positively from the Bible, he is in fact doing the greatest possible purifying and strengthening job for family life.

I have emphasized the negative, because my theme has been public policy and law. But the Christian layman who comes out of his church on a Sunday is a voter and a citizen, and we must hear his voice. He needs to ask his government to protect the family by law. In this cause, we must spend and be spent. That is how we demonstrate that we love our neighbour and our family, and that we want them all to be stable, secure and happy.

[34] Such a proposal forms a major part of discussion on parental roles in education initiated by the Government in 1988–9